VEGGIE MAMA

ALSO BY DOREEN VIRTUE AND JENNY ROSS

The Art of Raw Living Food

ALSO BY DOREEN VIRTUE

BOOKS/KITS/ORACLE BOARD

Awaken Your Indigo Power (with Charles Virtue)
The Courage to Be Creative
Nutrition for Intuition (with Robert Reeves, N.D.)
Don't Let Anything Dull Your Sparkle
Earth Angel Realms
Living Pain-Free (with Robert Reeves, N.D.)
The Big Book of Angel Tarot (with Radleigh Valentine)
Angels of Abundance (with Grant Virtue)
Angel Dreams (with Melissa Virtue)
Angel Astrology 101 (with Yasmin Boland)
Angel Detox (with Robert Reeves, N.D.)
Assertiveness for Earth Angels
How to Heal a Grieving Heart (with James Van Praagh)
The Essential Doreen Virtue Collection
The Miracles of Archangel Gabriel
Mermaids 101
Flower Therapy (with Robert Reeves, N.D.)
Mary, Queen of Angels
Saved by an Angel
The Angel Therapy® Handbook
Angel Words (with Grant Virtue)
Archangels 101
The Healing Miracles of Archangel Raphael
Signs from Above (with Charles Virtue)
The Miracles of Archangel Michael
Angel Numbers 101
Solomon's Angels (a novel)
My Guardian Angel (with Amy Oscar)
Angel Blessings Candle Kit (with Grant Virtue; includes booklet, CD, journal, etc.)
Thank You, Angels! (children's book with Kristina Tracy)
Healing Words from the Angels
How to Hear Your Angels
Fairies 101
Daily Guidance from Your Angels
Divine Magic
How to Give an Angel Card Reading Kit
Angels 101
Angel Guidance Board
Crystal Therapy (with Judith Lukomski)
Connecting with Your Angels Kit (includes booklet, CD, journal, etc.)
The Crystal Children
Archangels & Ascended Masters
Earth Angels

Messages from Your Angels
Angel Visions II
Eating in the Light (with Becky Black, M.F.T., R.D.)
The Care and Feeding of Indigo Children
Angel Visions
Divine Prescriptions
Healing with the Angels
"I'd Change My Life If I Had More Time"
Divine Guidance
Chakra Clearing
Angel Therapy®
Constant Craving A–Z
Constant Craving
The Yo-Yo Diet Syndrome
Losing Your Pounds of Pain

AUDIO/CD PROGRAMS

The Healing Miracles of Archangel Raphael (unabridged audio book)
Angel Therapy® Meditations
Archangels 101 (abridged audio book)
Solomon's Angels (unabridged audio book)
Fairies 101 (abridged audio book)
Angel Medicine (available as both 1- and 2-CD sets)
Angels among Us (with Michael Toms)
Messages from Your Angels (abridged audio book)
Past-Life Regression with the Angels
Divine Prescriptions
The Romance Angels
Connecting with Your Angels
Manifesting with the Angels
Karma Releasing
Healing Your Appetite, Healing Your Life
Healing with the Angels
Divine Guidance
Chakra Clearing

DVD PROGRAM

How to Give an Angel Card Reading

CALENDAR

Angel Affirmations (for each individual year)

CARD DECKS

Loving Words from Jesus
Butterfly Oracle Cards for Life Changes
Fairy Tarot Cards (with Radleigh Valentine)
Archangel Gabriel Oracle Cards
Angel Answers Oracle Cards (with Radleigh Valentine)
Past Life Oracle Cards (with Brian Weiss, M.D.)
Guardian Angel Tarot Cards (with Radleigh Valentine)
Cherub Angel Cards for Children
Talking to Heaven Mediumship Cards
(with James Van Praagh)
Archangel Power Tarot Cards (with Radleigh Valentine)
Flower Therapy Oracle Cards (with Robert Reeves, N.D.)
Indigo Angel Oracle Cards (with Charles Virtue)
Angel Dreams Oracle Cards (with Melissa Virtue)
Mary, Queen of Angels Oracle Cards

Angel Tarot™ Cards (with Radleigh Valentine
and Steve A. Roberts)
The Romance Angels Oracle Cards
Life Purpose Oracle Cards
Archangel Raphael Healing Oracle Cards
Archangel Michael Oracle Cards
Angel Therapy® Oracle Cards
Magical Messages from the Fairies Oracle Cards
Ascended Masters Oracle Cards
Daily Guidance from Your Angels Oracle Cards
Saints & Angels Oracle Cards
Magical Unicorns Oracle Cards
Goddess Guidance Oracle Cards
Archangel Oracle Cards
Magical Mermaids and Dolphins Oracle Cards
Messages from Your Angels Oracle Cards
Healing with the Fairies Oracle Cards
Healing with the Angels Oracle Cards

ALSO BY JENNY ROSS

BOOKS

Healing with Raw Foods
Simply Dehydrated
Raw Basics

All of the above are available at your local bookstore, or may be ordered through
Hay House USA: www.hayhouse.com®; Hay House Australia: www.hayhouse.com.au;
Hay House UK: www.hayhouse.co.uk; Hay House South Africa: www.hayhouse.co.za;
Hay House India: www.hayhouse.co.in

Doreen's website: www.AngelTherapy.com
Jenny's website: www.jennyrosslivingfoods.com

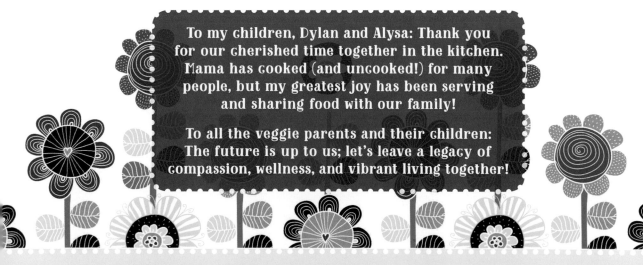

To my children, Dylan and Alysa: Thank you for our cherished time together in the kitchen. Mama has cooked (and uncooked!) for many people, but my greatest joy has been serving and sharing food with our family!

To all the veggie parents and their children: The future is up to us; let's leave a legacy of compassion, wellness, and vibrant living together!

♥ DOREEN VIRTUE & JENNY ROSS ♥

VEGGIE MAMA

A FUN, WHOLESOME GUIDE TO FEEDING
Your Kids Tasty Plant-Based Meals

HAY HOUSE, INC.
Carlsbad, California · New York City
London · Sydney · Johannesburg
Vancouver · New Delhi

Library of Congress Cataloging-in-Publication Data

Names: Virtue, Doreen, date, author. | Ross, Jenny, author.
Title: Veggie Mama : a fun, wholesome guide to feeding your kids tasty plant-based meals / Doreen Virtue and Jenny Ross.
Description: Carlsbad, California : Hay House, Inc., [2016] | Includes index.
Identifiers: LCCN 2016019782 | ISBN 9781401947491 (tradepaper : alk. paper)
Subjects: LCSH: Vegetarian cooking. | Children--Nutrition. | LCGFT: Cookbooks.
Classification: LCC TX837 .V5723 2016 | DDC 641.5/636--dc23
LC record available at https://lccn.loc.gov/2016019782

ISBN: 978-1-4019-4749-1

10 9 8 7 6 5 4 3 2 1

1st edition, September 2016

Printed in the United States of America

SUSTAINABLE FORESTRY INITIATIVE
Certified Sourcing
www.sfiprogram.org
SFI-01268
SFI label applies to text stock only

CONTENTS

Preface ix
Introduction.. xv

PART I: VEGGIE MAMA BASICS

CHAPTER 1: **Veggie Mama** Guiding Principles...3
CHAPTER 2: **Veggie Mama** Family Nutrition....................................13
CHAPTER 3: **Veggie Mama** Fresh Cart, Pantry, and Kitchen Setup...................27
CHAPTER 4: **Veggie Mama** Meal Planning...45

PART II: VEGGIE MAMA FAMILY-FRIENDLY RECIPES

CHAPTER 5: **Veggie Mama** Power-Up Breakfasts, Juice Selections, and Smoothies...57
CHAPTER 6: **Veggie Mama** Fresh and Fun Family Entrées
(Including Brown-Bag School Lunch Options)..........................99
CHAPTER 7: **Veggie Mama** Mix-and-Match Soups, Salads, Sauces, and Sides 121
CHAPTER 8: **Veggie Mama** Wholesome Sweet Treats and Desserts 163
CHAPTER 9: **Veggie Mama** "I'm Hungry" Go-To Snacks
and Nourishing Palate Pleasers 183
CHAPTER 10: **Veggie Mama** Adventures in Sprouted and Fermented Foods..........199
CHAPTER 11: **Veggie Mama** Kid-Party Platters and Plant-Powered Entertaining 215

Afterword.. 233
Appendix 235
  • *Vegan Preconception and Pregnancy Planning*
  • *Vegan Postpartum*
Metric Conversion Chart 246
Recipe Index 248
About the Authors 251

PREFACE

Although the title of this book is *Veggie Mama*, we definitely include Veggie Papas (and other key parental figures) under the umbrella of nurturing guardians who provide healthful meals for their children. As we continue through this Preface, you will learn a little bit about both of us Veggie Mamas writing this book and *how*—or rather, *when*—we began our commitment to raising plant-powered kids. Our stories are different, and together we hope to inspire, educate, and motivate your own steps closer to clean, whole, vegetarian foods as a foundation for your healthy family.

Doreen's Veggie Mama Story

My parents raised me and my younger brother with healthful food. My father has been a vegetarian since childhood. Very ill as a child, he was internally guided to give up eating animal products. As a result, he healed and has lived a very long and healthful life (he's approaching 90 years old now).

My mother was a food counselor with Weight Watchers when I was a child, so she cooked our family lots of low-fat food. She was very creative in making vegetarian fare that was low-cost. We were also on a tight budget after Dad had quit his aerospace engineering job in order to pursue his dream of making his passion for model airplanes into a home-based business. We ate healthfully, and Dad's business thrived and supported us.

In college, I studied both journalism and psychology. While pursuing my bachelor's degree in counseling psychology from Chapman University, I volunteered at a local alcoholism rehabilitation hospital. Eventually, they hired me as a counselor. That was a real eye-opening experience for me, because my family was and is sober. I learned about addictive family dynamics by working in the hospital.

A social worker at the hospital ran group therapy for those with eating disorders, and she offered to mentor me. I gratefully accepted, and found that I loved working with women who struggled with weight and eating issues.

A local psychiatrist offered to sponsor my opening my own eating disorders outpatient clinic, which I agreed to do. I had an office at his busy psychiatric building, where I saw eight clients per day for one-hour sessions each. I continued with college while working at this clinic and earned my master's degree in counseling psychology from Chapman University.

I noticed patterns among my clients, in which their cravings and binge-eating patterns corresponded with their emotional issues. I eventually wrote about this pattern in my book *Constant Craving*.

I transitioned from outpatient work to inpatient hospital work. First, I was an administrator at an all-women's psychiatric facility in Northern California called Woodside Women's Hospital. We treated women with a variety of issues. The hospital was so successful that I was offered a program director position at Cumberland Hall Hospital in Nashville, Tennessee, where I opened and ran an all-women unit called Woman-Kind in the 1990s.

By then, my writing and speaking career was so busy that I no longer could devote enough time to my clients. So I left hospital and outpatient practice so that I could write and speak full-time. I wrote *Losing Your Pounds of Pain* about my healing experiences with eating-disordered women who'd been abused in childhood. This same book was also the basis of my doctoral dissertation about the link between childhood abuses and the development of addictions.

Right after graduating with my Ph.D. in counseling psychology, I changed my family's diet to organic when my two sons were 13 and 15 years old. With my research in food and eating disorders, it was actually my intuition that guided me away from chemicals and genetically modified food.

I'd had a brush with death in 1995 that was a big wake-up call for me. I realized that, although I was successful as an eating-disorders therapist, I wasn't happy or fulfilled in that role. The reason why I'd had so many different jobs as a therapist was because I was searching for something that couldn't be found for me in that career.

I took a leap of faith and left psychology so that I could focus upon meditation, and studying, writing, and teaching about spirituality—particularly about angels. That's when I began receiving strong intuitive messages that led me to go vegan with organic food. I've been 100 percent vegan ever since.

I was amazed to discover how, within a month of eating organic, my sons transformed from typically hyper and aggressive boys into sweet and focused ones. The change was immediate and total, and it made sense because eating pesticides is literally ingesting a chemical that's used for the ultimate in aggressive behavior: killing pests. When I removed pesticides from their diets, my sons were no longer aggressive.

This coincided with a time when, in 1996, I began having visions of food.

While meditating, in my mind's eye, I could see images of what I commonly ate. It wasn't a conjuring image, like when you're hungry. These were spontaneous visuals of food, appearing as three-dimensional objects.

I had no idea why I was seeing this. It took me several months to realize that my food visions were answers to the question

I'd asked of God about how to increase my visual intuition.

I followed this visual guidance and changed my diet. Almost immediately, my visions vastly improved. It was like upgrading from a tiny television set to a high-definition large-screen! Suddenly, my visions were fully formed and more understandable.

Again following my guidance, I began teaching classes to help others awaken their spiritual abilities to see and feel guidance. I taught my students about the link between food and intuition, and many of them changed their diets, with outcomes similar to those I'd had.

I noticed that when I began feeding my children high-life-force food, especially organic food, their energy shifted. My two teenagers became sweeter and more loving, and developed an awareness of their emotional and physical well-being. Now that they're adults living on their own, they continue to eat healthfully.

I never pushed veganism on them. Instead, I fed them high-life-force foods. My sons made their own decision to continue eating in a way that made them feel good. Today, my eldest son, Charles, eats mostly vegetarian food with occasional fish, and my youngest, Grant, is a vegan. Both eat organic food and avoid chemicals, including genetically modified products, because I raised them to read labels and be aware of how foods affect their bodies.

Jenny's Veggie Mama Story

Children are such blessings. I enjoyed two healthy and vital vegan pregnancies. During my first pregnancy, everything was new to me, so I went to my obstetrician and I shared with him that I had a potentially unique dietary lifestyle that did not include animal proteins. I actually held back from oversharing, as I was unsure about his previous experience with vegan mothers or his nutritional understanding of a "raw" vegan diet. My intention was to address the subject of my then-"alternative" lifestyle without causing alarm. So I merely stated that I was vegetarian, explaining the raw component as simply as I could. He wasn't concerned for my health, although my dietary lifestyle was new to him, but he did make me promise to have my blood tested at every visit so that we could be sure I was getting enough nutrition for a pregnant mom. I consented, and five months into my pregnancy, he remarked, "Well, you are basically the healthiest mom in here," citing my living-plant-based diet as a welcome and balanced approach to nutrition during my pregnancy. He laid off the blood tests after that!

With Dylan, my first, I worked until the day before he was born. Being a raw-foods chef during both my pregnancies, I put in rather long and strenuous days in my own restaurants during this important time in my life. So it was even more encouraging to me that my dietary lifestyle allowed me to keep up and maintain energy throughout my final trimester.

Over the last two decades, following an initial health crisis, I have been very fortunate to enjoy a lifestyle full of fresh living foods. When I healed my body through raw foods and yoga, I became very passionate and purposeful. It was clear to me that my calling was to help others find healing for their own bodies. I quickly learned about how to create delicious raw foods in my own kitchen out of necessity, and then I was guided by Spirit to open a restaurant for others to begin experiencing the healing power of raw foods. That pursuit of my passion led to my meeting Doreen and our collaboration on the book *The Art of Raw Living Foods* (Hay House, 2009). Teaching about and creating raw-foods dishes has been my life! During the downtime between my children's births, I furthered my education with a degree in holistic nutrition. Since then, I have shared the opportunity for health through plant-based nutrition with clients around the globe, and I've found everyone has the same desire: to experience vibrant wellness! In fact, in my previous book, *Healing with Raw Foods* (Hay House, 2015), I partnered with several doctors to create a manual for using raw foods as the basis for healing, as a direct response to what I saw as a global need for deeper information about the powers of raw foods and how to harness them.

Three years after I gave birth to my son, Dylan, my daughter, Alysa, was born. I again was strong, focused, and in control of the natural order of things in my body. I highly recommend balanced plant-based eating for pregnancy, especially with a solid base of whole, living raw foods for the extra enzymes and nutrient value.

I hope that every woman bringing life into the world will have the opportunity to experience such bliss in her own life, as I have been forever gifted and changed by these two miracles. I know as a result of committing to a clean, healthy, plant-strong diet full of fresh living foods my body was ready for this incredible experience, and I know that it can be a powerful force for *all* women.

♥

Making the simple and delicious recipes in this book will help you carry out a commitment toward vibrant living for the whole family. In a world of tremendous distraction, nutritious, plant-based food is a great gift for your loved ones, because it's the basis of the ongoing gift of health. *Feeding* your children healthfully starts their lifetime habit of *eating* healthfully.

Families thrive on balanced plant-based foods. Your renewed commitment year after year to developing a dietary lifestyle that evolves as each member's needs change leads to powerful results. Benefits range from enhanced immunity, meaning less impact from cold-and-flu season on your household, to increased energy, meaning happier and more beneficial patterns throughout the day (think about getting your kids up for school in the morning and finding them more balanced and energized, and you're on the right track!). When vibrant health is the center of your family's experience, you reconnect with the simple joys in life!

Your choice in favor of healthful foods may be the decision that catapults your family life into the extraordinary. May your journey be unique, just as you are, and filled with unexpected gifts . . . and may you and your loved ones enjoy vibrant health in every way!

With love,
The Veggie Mamas,
Doreen and Jenny
xoxo

♥ ♥ ♥

→ · INTRODUCTION · ←

There is something incredibly powerful about choosing whole, plant food nutrition for yourself and your loved ones, which is evident in daily habits as well as the opportunity for long-term wellness.

This single choice can create a foundation for your family members that will promote vibrant health of the body, mind, and spirit for a lifetime. Plant-based foods are naturally supportive of the immune system, delivering all the essential building blocks of life. Whole, plant-powered meals, like those we Veggie Mamas are here to share, are complete, nutrient dense, and full of vital enzymes, with no additives or denatured foods that leave behind toxins in the body. Thus, the Veggie Mama philosophy is one of "clean foods," as described here, that will help build the strongest bodies, free of disease. As an added bonus, Veggie Mama recipes are naturally energizing, so you can power your best life with the vital fuel to create an extraordinary future.

As you embark on a journey toward the greater health of your family, be sure to take things one day at a time. As your road map, this book will walk you through daily plant-strong living for yourself and your loved ones. Eventually you can easily manage a week's worth of meals using the tools and recipes included in these pages, and hopefully that will blossom into a lifestyle of living well on plant-based cuisine for you and your family. From the moment you begin, the benefit of these choices will be tangible and obvious in some ways—potentially, you will find increased energy or a break from the tantrums that follow a meal of unhealthy food!

The Veggie Mama Philosophy

The Veggie Mama philosophy is not an all-or-nothing approach to eating. It is an *abundant* approach to food that will leave you feeling strong and satiated. Throughout this book, you will find an assortment of recipes that include many varying options for personal enjoyment, with choices for different toppings or cooking techniques. Many of the recipes are considered "raw-foods" dishes. There are also some "transitional" vegan recipes that can be further modified to support you as you're taking steps to help transition family members to the enjoyment of living plant foods in their most natural state.

Here is a basic understanding of how these recipes and their benefits differ:

Raw Foods

Raw foods have been heated to 118°F max to preserve the vital nutrients. Raw-foods dishes offer the most available nutrient density and are also high in water content and enzyme activity—the catalysts for all bodily functions. They are the simplest foods on the planet. We have created some recipes that can take these simple foods and turn them into delicious full entrées, snacks, and desserts to please even the pickiest eaters. We have marked all raw recipes and raw components with a RAW designation so they are easy to find as you scan through the book.

Transitional Vegan Foods

Transitional recipes contain some cooked whole foods, like quinoa and rice, and they are just that—perfect for transition. Typically served warmer, they will still incorporate some raw elements. These dishes are all still plant based and utilize whole-foods ingredients.

As you experience more fresh foods in your dietary lifestyle, you may naturally gravitate toward the physical and energetic differences these foods provide. Every parent and child is created with a unique chemistry set—the human body! Some family members may enjoy the grounding and warming effects of transitional foods, while others may flourish entirely on raw foods. The more raw foods in the diet, the better, though, when it comes to packing in nutritional density.

Think of "energy in equals energy out"! However, some people need to gradually transition their diet so that they can still *enjoy* eating and keep it as a healthy, vital part of their experience of life. As a veggie parent, you will find your kids' preferences to be obvious.

The key is to stay in communication with your family regarding their food and to take note of what supports your children in each stage of life. For this, your intuition plays an important role. Along with the knowledge of the body's essential needs for nutrient intake at each stage of development, your intuition will help you create the best meal plan possible for your own unique family.

The Manual for Life, One Bite at a Time!

As a general guide, *Veggie Mama* is a manual for elevating your family's diet to include more whole plant-based foods. While both raw and transitional vegan options are 100 percent plant based, recipes here use **whole ingredients only**. We do not advocate processed foods made "in a plant" (even if they originate "from a plant"), which could contain shelf-stabilizing enhancers or additives that don't benefit human health. Instead, we include whole grains, legumes, nuts, seeds, fruits, and vegetables in this approach, along with superfoods—whole foods that provide a large health benefit in a small package.

Additionally, this book has been created with **acid-alkaline balance** in mind. In my (Jenny's) previous book *Healing with Raw Foods*, the connection between an alkaline diet and wellness is explained as an incredible force for healing the body. We know that disease cannot "live" in an alkaline environment, so we have worked to create balance in every dish here for the best possible health result. Alkaline diets lower inflammation and have been indicated in powerfully working to support the body in reducing overall histamine reactions to food and environmental toxins.

If your child is allergy sensitive, attention to acid-alkaline ratios could help support his or her body in finding better balance. Please take a look at the chart on pages 20–21 to see which foods are more alkaline forming. You are looking to create *balance*, so if you enjoy an acidic food component in a meal, be sure to balance it with something alkaline forming. The more alkaline foods you add into the diet, the better, considering that stress and environmental toxins are themselves all acid forming. Veggie Mamas report green smoothies are a great tool for this; try one of the alkaline-forming smoothie recipes in Chapter 4 for breakfast or an afternoon snack and watch the results. You are aiming to have a balanced pH of 7.2 or an alkaline pH of up to 8.0 for optimal health.

We will discuss food allergies in this book, as well as some common dietary concerns for growing families. With this in mind, the Veggie Mama approach is also a **CSG-free** program—meaning free of corn, soy (with the exception of fermented miso paste), and gluten. Processed soy (in the case of tofu, for instance), gluten, and corn are all inflammatory foods that can create anxiety for sensitive kids, as well as worsen allergic symptoms.

Although we take an abundant approach to eating, we abide by the idea of "when in doubt, leave it out" when it comes to your and your family's best health. As our food resources evolve, if you are uncertain about what a product is or what it contains, be sure to check it out before adding it to your shopping cart and into your daily food lifestyle. To keep current with us on all the emerging health news, you can join the Veggie Mama online community at Facebook .com/jennyrosslivingfoods.

"Where Do I Start?"

In this book, we have laid out the chapters with the informational pieces, the "how-to" of the Veggie Mama kitchen, in Part I, followed by chapters of recipes that also include a wealth of nutritional information. If you are brand-new to plant-based and whole-foods eating, we recommend reading the introductory chapters first to familiarize yourself with the ingredients, tools, and more!

Once you become more confident in the kitchen, you can literally grab this book and flip to any chapter to prepare balanced and nutrient-dense menus for your family. For preconception- and pregnancy-specific information, we have included a special section for you to consult in the Appendix. And there are easy go-to charts throughout for your reference as your needs and the needs of your family evolve.

♥ ♥ ♥

PART I
VEGGIE MAMA
Basics

Chapter 1

VEGGIE MAMA
GUIDING PRINCIPLES

By definition, *Veggie Mama* is a plant-strong, vegetarian culture and dietary lifestyle comprising whole foods, prepared in a loving way, for the highest and best nutrient value. This book includes a variety of vegan recipes and important information so that you can feel confident that your family members are meeting all their nutritional needs, while enjoying what may be an entirely new food choice.

"Veggie Mama" is the idea that as a parent, you can fully own and inspire your family's plant-based food choices. When you are all-in on something great, the motivation to keep it up, to spread the word with your friends, and to advocate on behalf of your passion is high! As two authors who have loved becoming Veggie Mamas and sharing this opportunity with our friends and family, we are equally enthusiastic about sharing it here with you today!

The Veggie Mama lifestyle was born of necessity for both of us. You know when what you are currently doing no longer serves you and it's time to upgrade your reality. We've both shared our personal stories with you in the Preface and will continue to do so throughout this book, but here especially we want to outline what we hope for *you*.

Nourish

The Veggie Mama lifestyle is about *nourishing* your family deeply, from the inside out, building the lives and bodies of healthy children and adults through quality nutrition. For this reason, we advocate ingredients that are not only "clean" and "whole" but also nutrient dense. We will show you throughout this book how to take a simple ingredient and retain its wholesome quality while at the same time making sure it tastes great—so your evolving home food culture can revolve around the joy of eating delicious meals.

Thrive

When your family enjoys fresh, whole plant-based foods, it's possible for their health to be catapulted and everyone to thrive! We've both seen this in our own lives, and it's the opportunity for any Veggie Mama who commits to making healthy food choices for her family, especially using the tools and ideas presented in this book.

There may be a number of reasons you are considering a change in dietary lifestyle, but for many families, the choice comes down to a desire for better health and greater vitality. This simple lifestyle can get you there quickly!

Share

Sharing health and wellness with others is a natural result of experiencing the benefits in your own life. Both of us have so much to share because those benefits have been *tremendous* in our families: from increased energy, to improved focus, to overcoming challenges related to food allergies and intolerances, to relief from common colds. From personally achieving these results and having families with strong immune systems, we have cataloged ways to use these powerful food choices to better the daily life of *any* family.

We know that once you understand and experience these potent changes in your own kitchen, you will naturally encourage others to take the steps necessary to experience them for themselves. That's what it's all about! A healthy family shares and builds a healthy community that can positively impact the world! A shift in food consciousness is under way, and whether you are taking part because you've felt a gentle tugging on your heart to eat foods that are more sustainable for the planet, or you are looking into a health opportunity and realizing the important role food can play in the prevention and reversal of disease, we know that what we share can benefit *you* . . . and what you go on to share will benefit another.

Going Deeper:
The Good, the Bad,
and the Opportunity

Veggie Mamas are all about nourishing their families with healthy foods that are free of additives and toxins. Our mantra is to provide nutritionally dense options that will build healthy brains and bodies and activate a spirit of joy in our homes. This means using organic foods and learning about the origin of food ingredients so that we can be the gatekeepers of wellness in our households.

The Good: The Importance of Organics

Organic foods are generally free of synthetic pesticides, which contain harmful toxins, and are handled from farm to store among organic products of a similar nature, preventing transference from other foods. Because organic produce is usually grown in smaller quantities and requires more maintenance than conventional food, its price is generally higher. However, we feel strongly that organics are an important investment in your family's health, and the health of the planet your children are inheriting.

It may not always be possible to find an organic version of everything in a recipe. So, when faced with a decision of what to buy that has the *least* amount of potential toxins, we recommend consulting a website like the Environmental Working Group (www.ewg .org) or a smartphone app such as:

- True Food
- The Non-GMO Project Shopping Guide
- The Healthy Food, Allergens, GMOs & Nutrition Scanner

All of the above are available in your App Store.

The Environmental Working Group's website has a list of the "clean 15" and the "dirty dozen" foods, which is updated annually to keep up with agricultural practices.

Crops and plants with thin skins susceptible to pests are more heavily sprayed, while tree fruits and plants with thick skins have less need for pesticides. In this case, a banana that is not organic is a relatively safer choice than a strawberry or an apple. The same with vegetables, especially those that grow in the ground—for these, it's really best to get organic as often as possible.

The Bad: The Rise in GMOs and Allergies

Another important sourcing note relates to genetically modified organisms or genetically engineered crops (GMO or GEC), which have pesticides and herbicides built into the foods themselves instead of manually sprayed on top . . . guaranteeing ingestion of toxins.

The top genetically modified foods are:

- Corn (including corn oil, corn syrup, and vitamin C supplements made from corn)
- Soy (including soybean oil, edamame, and tofu)
- Sugar beets
- Aspartame (also known as NutraSweet)
- Papayas from Hawaii
- Rice
- Bananas
- Salmon
- Peas
- Alfalfa

- Honey
- Wheat
- Tomatoes
- Canola oil
- Zucchini
- Yellow squash
- Beets
- Yeast
- Dairy (because cows and goats are fed GMO feed, and the toxins are passed through the milk, along with harmful antibiotics and growth hormones)
- Meats (again, because animals are fed GMO food, and the toxins are present in their bodies)
- Cotton (including cottonseed oil)

For the preceding foods, it is especially important to buy only organic, non-GMO varieties. In the case of aspartame, natural raw sweeteners are the best alternative.

Tragically, there's an increasing link between these foods and allergies. Genetic modification itself may not always be labeled, so we recommend you stay aware and look for "non-GMO" labeled ingredients wherever possible, or use one of the phone apps listed previously.

A note about food allergies and sensitivities: As we will discuss in the next chapter, food allergies are on the rise in both children and adults. In fact, they are more prevalent today than even one decade ago,

and the Centers for Disease Control and Prevention (CDC) reports that they increased by *50 percent* between 1997 and 2011. One of the suspected culprits accounting for this increase, although no specific links have been proven in main clinical trials, has to do with the farming and cultivation practices for these key crops. The general overuse of these foods in modern diets also has the potential for resulting in resistance, as well as the cultivation of genetic markers associated with food allergy and other autoimmune challenges. What that means is that when our bodies are overexposed to these foods, we become resistant to them, often developing food intolerances as well as triggering the body's own DNA sequences to set off potential changes to our genetic makeup as a response to an overburdened immune system. This specific reaction has been implicated in many autoimmune issues in the body, such as the thyroid condition known as Hashimoto's, lupus, and some types of cancer.

The good news is that a balanced Veggie Mama diet is naturally free of many of these allergens. Once your diet is primarily based around whole plant foods, it leaves little room for any of the common allergens with the exception of nuts. (Nuts are easy to work around, because seeds will provide many of the same health benefits and in some cases even more.)

If you or your child is histamine-intolerant (please see the next chapter and Chapter 10 for more information on this), then you'll need to eliminate vinegar, pickled or fermented products, avocado, spinach, and papaya from your recipe ingredients.

The Opportunity: Food as Medicine— Veggie Mama Special Considerations

If you need to work with specialized diets in your home, there is tribe of individuals in every community who can support you, from your pediatrician to other integrated practitioners focusing on acupuncture, chiropractic, kinesiology, and holistic nutrition. Treatment through nutrition is a common focus with alternative practitioners. We eat three to five times a day, so using plant medicine is an obvious choice when looking to naturally heal the body. Every meal is an opportunity to throw the body out of balance . . . or to *recenter* the body. We can powerfully support our children and their best health, especially when dealing with autism, ADD/ADHD, behavioral issues, and autoimmune deficiencies by focusing on the nutritional cure.

— **Autism, ADD, and ADHD.** Autism has been consistently on the rise, affecting 1 in 68 children in 2014 in America. According to the National Autism Association, *autism* can be defined as "a bio-neurological developmental disability that generally appears before the age of three." This affects the areas of the brain relative to communication, social interaction, ability to concentrate, and critical thinking. Autism can be greatly impacted and managed with a dietary focus.

Overall a dairy-free, gluten-free meal plan that is alkaline forming is key to the dietary treatment of autism. The reduced inflammation and "clean-burning fuel" can allow a child who suffers at the low end of the autism spectrum to live virtually symptom-free. Those on the high end may also see improvement if they keep to a strict diet and a closer look is taken at environmental toxins that can lead to inflammation. ADD and ADHD are similarly impacted by food.

The blessing here is that you can ensure the overall health of your entire family while at the same time using powerful tools to overcome specific symptoms in an individual member. Alkaline diets prevent disease and are the best supporters of the immune system. The foods and programs we have laid out in this book are all naturally alkalizing!

— **Autoimmune deficiencies.** As our world is inundated with unnatural materials and experiences, the incidence of autoimmune deficiencies, like celiac disease, type 1 diabetes, and lupus, is becoming more prevalent in children. Dietary choices can greatly impact the stress put on a child's body by a number of the different autoimmune deficiencies we see. In total, a diet complete with a nutrient-dense menu and balanced meals that are also free from inflammatory foods, like gluten and dairy, is a good choice for children dealing with autoimmune issues.

Many children with type 1 diabetes who are insulin dependent see a sharp decrease in the amount of insulin needed when they switch to a plant-based diet. Dr. Gabriel Cousens has been researching the body's ability to "cure" diabetes for more than a decade at his Tree of Life facility in Patagonia, Arizona, and had seen tremendous results, including complete health reversals for type 2 diabetics. Type 1 insulin-dependent diabetics who adopt a plant-based, living-foods diet are in many cases able to release 80 to 100 percent of their insulin dependency as well. There is hope, and science supports children and adults choosing clean, whole plant-based foods for wellness. In fact, diet has been shown to be the leading factor in healing diabetic conditions.

Making the "Midlife" Switch to Being a Veggie Mama Family

The challenge—or, as we prefer to think of it, the opportunity—we hear often from Veggie Mamas goes back to the question of "how" to transition kids who were not raised on clean foods, or whole foods, let alone vegan foods. The answer to this is unique to your individual family, but here are a couple of tips from those who have gone through it.

1. **Focus on adding.** Add something new each week that is 100 percent vegan, clean, and whole that is similar to something else your family enjoys. If they love broccoli with creamy sauce, for example, simple switch out the cream for an avocado or tahini sauce, and add that in somewhere in their meal plan for the week.

2. **Enroll your children in helping you research recipes for the family to try, and ask them to help you make them.** Kids of all ages are proud of the foods they enjoy. I (Jenny) have learned through the homeschool classes I teach that the kids in attendance will try foods in class that would normally daunt them because they are surrounded by peers and also because they had a hand in preparing them.

3. **Lead with encouragement.** Studies show that kids who are required to try something, even if it's for a reward, are less likely to enjoy the foods they are forced to try. Lead instead from a space of encouragement, offering a wider variety of healthy foods often, and don't give up! You may have to present an item multiple times before your child will trust it enough to take a bite.

Getting Everyone on Board

As I (Doreen) mentioned in the Preface, when my two sons were young teenagers, I was guided to switch them (and myself) to an organic plant-based diet. This was in 1996, before Whole Foods and similar health-food superstores were prevalent.

Although Charles and Grant were energetic teenagers with strong wills (and friends who ate junk food), the switch to a plant-based diet was harmonious and effortless. I credit the following actions for the smooth transition to healthful eating for my sons:

— **Benefits-oriented discussions.** Before making the switch, my family had meetings to discuss the reasons for the switch. We talked about the health benefits of avoiding pesticides and animal cruelty. The focus upon benefits helped Charles and Grant look for the positive aspects, instead of focusing upon the foods they were "giving up."

You can watch YouTube videos with your family, showing the benefits of switching to an organic, non-GMO, plant-based diet. Many of the YouTube videos are cartoons meant to help children understand the basis of eating organic vegetables and fruits. Children also love to watch the TED and TEDx videos that feature other children giving speeches about organics.

— **Emphasis upon flavor.** Family members may initially resist a plant-based diet if they believe it will consist of boring salads and plain vegetables. The good news is that you can make virtually any traditional recipe into a plant-based version. In many cases, the plant-based version tastes superior to the traditional recipe! Or your family may not even be able to tell the difference.

— **Easy does it.** We gradually transitioned away from meat by moving to a plant-based diet supplemented with wild-caught fish (which is much healthier for the planet and our bodies than farm-raised fish). If your family is accustomed to eating red meat, you might switch at first to chicken- or turkey-based dishes, then to fish-based ones, and then wean off of animal products altogether. Fortunately, there are so many delicious meat substitutes available now. Just make sure that if you use soy products, they are certified non-GMO (which is largely proclaimed on the product's label). The next transition is away from cooked products into more *raw* plant-based meals.

— **Snacks.** Since children face junk-food temptations at school, in their friends' homes, and on television commercials, it's important to provide healthful alternatives. The recipes in this book include yummy snacks. If you involve your children in the creation of snacks, and even ask them to creatively add their own favorite (non-junk-food) ingredients, they will respond even more favorably to healthful snacks.

— **Involvement in meal planning and shopping.** Once a week, have a family meeting about which meals to serve during the week. You could even make one day of the week "Johnnie's favorites," the next day "Mary's favorites," and then "Dad's favorites," and so on, so that each family member gets excited about choosing the meal plan for that day.

Meal planning is also timesaving, because you can shop once or twice a week instead of every day. Taking the children to the store to help you select which head of organic broccoli they like the best, for instance, further involves them in the process. This increases their likelihood of appreciating and enjoying the meals.

Although organics and healthier foods are usually more expensive, I taught my children that this was an investment. We cut back on buying nonessentials so that we could afford good organic foods.

— **Self-monitoring.** You can motivate children to eat healthier by teaching them to monitor how they feel after they eat or drink. For example, I would ask my sons to tune in to their physical feelings while they were making smoothies together. Then I would ask them to notice how they felt while drinking their smoothies, and afterward. Of course they felt wonderful, because healthful smoothies are natural energy and mood boosters. Now that my sons are grown adults, they still choose to drink healthful smoothies and eat healthfully.

— **Rewards for healthful choices.** When I switched my sons to organic plant-based meals, I also taught them to read labels of foods and beverages before consuming them. I taught them how to identify and avoid any foods or drinks containing preservatives, additives, and other chemicals. I then rewarded them with one dollar for each day that they stayed away from eating or drinking anything containing chemicals. They proudly would tell me their stories of reading labels, and I was happy to spend $30 a month on each of them for this valuable life lesson. To this day, as adults, they continue to read labels and are conscious shoppers and consumers.

— **Healthful pantry and refrigerator.** I remember being a guest expert on the *Ricki Lake* television show when the topic was children who wanted to eat healthier and lose weight. The show featured a panel of mothers and their overweight preteen kids. Each of the children complained to their mothers that their refrigerators and cupboards contained only fattening junk food. One girl began crying, saying that she really wanted to eat vegetables, but there weren't any in the house. The mother promised to start buying produce.

I found that when I precut organic produce and then placed the pieces in colanders or bowls on eye-level shelves in the refrigerator, my sons would happily reach for apples, carrots, and other healthful snacks.

If you have a strong-willed child who resists giving up junk food, he or she may have formed a physical or psychological addiction to the ingredients, which usually stems from allergies and sensitivities. Also, some children and adults resist change and don't like to be told what to do. Power struggles rarely work. However, it *is* your home, and you have the right to eliminate junk food from your cupboards and refrigerator. Making it inconvenient for your child to obtain junk food does help.

Other Veggie Mama Challenges

A common challenge is the need to provide variety. When you are busy and confronted with life's day-to-day stressors, it can be easy to fall into food ruts. Our recommendation would be to commit to trying one new fruit or vegetable each week as an exploration of plant-based eating. Kids can get involved and learn about its cultivation, origin, and health benefits, adding to their understanding plant-based medicine through food.

Another challenge could be packing the lunch to go to school. You need some good, simple combinations your children will enjoy that can evolve as they grow. See our chart in Chapter 6 for practical ways to fill your veggie-kid lunch box. Also, while you are shopping, you may want to grab some lightweight stainless-steel refillable containers, or mason jars for older children, for easy grab-and-go storage of your recipes.

However, your choice to maintain a clean, plant-based lifestyle may require a bit more planning depending on the resources readily obtainable in your area. The ingredients you will source for your family may be sold only at specialty stores or online depending on your location. One of the first steps you can take is creating a list of local grocery stores or farmers' markets to check out in order to source your ingredients.

In this chapter, we outlined some of the joyous aspects of "veggie" parenting as well as diving right into the issues that, frankly, prevent families from making this transition. Even if your family containsresistant or picky eaters, you can learn to incorporate Veggie Mama foods simply by focusing on *adding* some of these great recipes to your table. Our hope for you is that your kids will be able to come together in this process and learn to fall in *love* with the amazing gifts of plant-based foods as they form a foundation for the optimal health of your family! We know you're a dedicated Veggie Mama (or Papa) or you wouldn't have picked up this book. Now it's time to hit the ground running and live it!

♥ ♥ ♥

Chapter 2

Veggie Mama Family Nutrition

At every age and stage of life, children have different caloric needs. Each phase of development requires its own set of resources from the body in order to foster the best possible health. With that said, growing healthy kids is simple, as proper nutrition is easy to navigate once you discover some basics to keep in mind. Keeping a watchful Veggie Mama eye on nutrient requirements is a necessary step for your children—not different than for any other mom.

Ages and Stages

(In the Appendix, you will find resources for newly pregnant as well as postpartum Veggie Mamas. During these magical times of creating and fostering life, these chapters can support your best nutrition and provide encouragement.)

Nutrition Ages 0 to 2

The World Health Organization (WHO) and UNICEF recommend exclusive breast-feeding from one hour after birth through six months of age. During this time, there should not be any need to supplement your baby with water, juice, or formula as long as feeding is done at regular intervals. Breast milk provides all the essential building blocks for babies to grow a healthy body and brain, and to support the vital-organ development that takes place in the first year of life.

Health experts now also agree that babies should be nursed as soon as they show signs of hunger. If breast-feeding is not an option, a healthy, plant-based formula should be prepared, ideally a formula that is not based in soy and has low sugars from natural sources. (Soy is high in phytoestrogens—which, although natural, could create hormonal imbalances in children.)

From six months to one year, solids can be slowly introduced into a baby's diet. Begin with simple foods, like the blended smoothies found in this book, fresh fruit, and easily digestible vegetables. You many also wish to incorporate almond mylk or hemp mylk into their diet as a way to provide additional healthy fats. Even so, according to WHO, it is effective to breast-feed for up to 24 months as the immune system is still developing and from there for as long as the nursing pair naturally desires.

A baby's brain *requires* healthy fat content. For this reason, nut butters, coconut, avocado, and hemp seeds are all simple and delicious foods your baby will likely grow to love from ages one to two. It's common for kids at this stage to eat small meals often, and therefore, you may want to keep little containers of simple, healthy foods like blueberries at the ready for grab-and-go snacking. Depending on their size and activity levels, toddlers should be enjoying nutrient-dense calories ranging from 1,000 to 1,400 per day. By the time you get into a routine of wellness with your baby, you'll find that it's easy and natural to feed your toddler right. During this stage, they will have quickly developed a taste for healthy, natural foods, as well as grown accustomed to the rituals associated with their preparation. For example, a welcome routine is a daily blended smoothie that can be shared with the whole family.

In general, toddlers should be enjoying 3 to 4 ounces of clean, plant-based protein daily, plus 3 to 4 cups of fresh fruits and vegetables. An additional 1 to 2 cups of grains, according to their size and whether or not they are still breast-feeding, are also recommended. Quinoa and rice are good starter grains.

Nutrition Ages 2 to 4

Once your child is further into the toddler stage, food exploration becomes a full-time occupation. Food trays, or ice-cube trays with multiple slots featuring different types of food, are a good way to introduce fresh fruits and vegetables with a fun presentation and also make sure your child is finding balance. If your child is still breast-feeding during this stage, 25 percent of their energy needs will be coming directly from the breast milk. You will want to fill the rest of their caloric needs—up to 1,600 calories a day, depending on their weight and size—with a variety of fresh foods rounded out with high-protein carbohydrates, like quinoa.

In general, 4 to 5 ounces of clean, plant-strong proteins a day should be mixed with 4 cups of fresh fruits and vegetables. Make sure your selections include many different colors and textures. Fresh water to keep hydrated is another consideration as your child is weaned off formula and breast milk. Additionally, 1 to 2 cups of grains should keep your vegan child healthy and strong.

Many Veggie Mamas are concerned that their children may not be getting enough of the essential nutrients in this important period of development. A couple of things to keep in mind during this time of increased growth:

1. **Your child should be enjoying a variety of fresh greens daily.** You may want to create a green smoothie for them to enjoy. You can serve it in a dark cup or a cup with a character on it if they are sensitive to the color. This liquid nutrition will help keep your child alkalized and ensure that additional calcium and iron will be available for creating healthy bones and muscles.

2. **A healthy growing brain needs clean, pure sources of essential fatty acids.** Be sure to incorporate those fats in a fun way—for example, by adding nut or seed butters to fruits and vegetables for between-meal snacks. Also try sprinkling some seeds—particularly pumpkin, watermelon, hemp, and sunflower seeds, which all contain more than 12 grams of protein per serving along with the omega fatty acids—over an entrée dish.

Little hands love to be involved at this stage! Working with your kids on projects that fit their motor abilities, like healthy vegan cookies, smoothies, and simple entrées, can help further their love of food preparation. As you prepare recipes safely and effectively, you will also add to their confidence in the kitchen and continue to cement the neuronal pathways that ascribe value—and, of course, fun!—to a healthy lifestyle.

Nutrition Ages 4 to 6

During this stage, kids are typically getting involved in school and working more with peers in learning groups. As a result, this is a wonderful opportunity to bolster their immune system with essentials, like probiotics and some fermented foods, from here on out. Probiotics are a great way to combat cold-and-flu season naturally. This is also a stage when locking down a food routine can be very helpful for the busy Veggie Mama. By now you understand the balance required in your children's diet. They will need the same ratios of protein to healthy carbohydrates (1:4) and essential fats as in early years; their serving sizes will just gradually get larger.

Calcium and iron continue to play a key role in further development during this stage. Now that your child's desire for taste and texture has evolved, you will want to try a variety of green foods to satisfy this mineral requirement. Sample ingredients like sea vegetables, sprouts, and chopped kale, as well as calcium-rich tahini and nut butters.

Nutrition Ages 6 to 12

As your children are assimilated in more group-learning environments, their food foundations have hopefully been laid with a bevy of fresh, nutrient-rich foods. However, if you are transitioning school-age children to a vegan lifestyle, you will have to slowly rework their mind-set with respect to food. This is a naturally peer-oriented stage in a child's life, so you really see how "social" eating begins to influence their dietary preferences.

More than ever, you will have to be creative with food, being extra mindful of the visual appeal. The selection of the ingredients will emphasize flavor and texture at this stage so that you can be sure the foods are interesting enough to catch their attention!

Our Cheesy Cauliflower (page 156) was born of this very need! One family I (Jenny) worked with in the 16-week whole-foods class I teach annually included an 8-year-old and a 13-year-old transitioning to a vegan lifestyle. The family kept running into challenges ensuring proper nutrition while coaxing the kids into the healthier fare. Many processed foods are so high in salt and fat that when humans try to shift away from these foods, they can feel loss because these pleasure points in the brain are not being triggered in the same fashion as before. During this transition, for adults and children alike, it is helpful to present foods that the mind sees as pleasurable. The introduction of a flavor that seemed familiar, in this case, the "cheese," combined with an entirely new base—a head of cauliflower—made the change appealing enough for this family to give it a try!

The National Institutes of Health suggests 1,400 to 1,800 calories per day, depending on activity level, height, and weight, during this stage. Again, the key thing here is to be sure your child is enjoying enough vital foods each day from each necessary category to sustain vibrant health.

Vegan kids will naturally eat more often during this stage than their friends who enjoy denser proteins. This is perfectly normal and stimulates their metabolism, setting it at a healthy rate, leading into prepubescence. If your child is not totally vegan, but rather is in transition and still enjoying a mix of foods, we recommend that you continue to focus on adding in more and more of the Veggie Mama basics, and as a matter of course, the other foods will slowly begin to fade away. It is important to tap into your children's mental connection to food, because healthy eating will need to be associated with positive enjoyment in order to support a positive relationship with food.

Simply switching out some of the sauces in your menu preparations, as well as your go-to desserts, can help you create new habits and new, healthier "food cravings" during these sometimes-formidable years. You can cut back on a lot of the potential processed food and refined sugars your kids are faced with just by focusing on these two categories. More often than not, your kids are like you: They are fascinated by the "idea" of a certain type of food. For example, a family member may be attached to the idea of prepared pasta, so changing the sauce and adding in a vegetable or two might be an easier step than removing this food altogether. If you can work on the smaller subtle changes first, it will be easier to eventually win over their palates on the larger issues.

Nutrition Ages 12 to 18

In the preteen and teenage years, it requires finesse to help your children make more and more of their own food choices. The natural independence that develops throughout this stage allows for eating apart from the family unit. It's helpful sometimes to support adolescents' process by asking them to check in to how they feel after food choices that may not be healthy or balanced.

It is a critical time, and their caloric needs will range from 1,800 to 2,400 a day, which means the option for consuming more varieties of foods, as well as potentially overindulging with processed foods. The CDC cites that the rate of childhood obesity has risen more than 400 percent in the last 30 years. From ages 10 to 18, important food habits are formed, and it is estimated that in America, one in three children during this stage of life will have a body mass index that is considered overweight. This unfortunate statistic is setting the next generation up for an adult population where one in two people is dealing with heart disease, diabetes, or cancer, along with other associated health concerns, like asthma and hypertension, which develop as a side effect of obesity. You can see how important it will be to ensure your family is enjoying an abundance of clean, plant-strong foods by this point in their lives!

An important special consideration for the teen years is watching the number of calories taken in from sugar. In both young men and women during this stage, the hormonal balance is shifting, and the endocrine system is sensitive to blood-sugar balance. When out of balance, sugar, because of its rapid uptake into the bloodstream and metabolism in the brain, can affect children's mood and ability to focus, hampering attention and leading to poor decision making. In fact, a UCLA study showed that students' ability to learn and retain information was negatively impacted by diets steadily high in fructose. Omega-3s, when introduced into the diet at the same time as abstaining from sugars, were able to counteract this effect. Acne is also a natural part of the teen stage, and the best way to combat it is to rely on low-glycemic, fresh foods and limited gluten-free grains for base nutrition.

Utilize some of the dessert recipes in this book to create treats made with natural sweeteners instead of processed sugars. This one choice can support your teen in confidently performing in learning settings with optimal concentration, as well as promote growth of healthy hair, skin, and nails.

General Guidelines for Veggie Mama Nutrition at All Stages!

Here are some basics that you can keep in mind when feeding family members of any age. The Veggie Mama philosophy is rooted in the best nutrition to optimally nourish the body, mind, and spirit. These guidelines are powerful principles we have seen play out positively with our own families over the years, and we hope they will help build confidence for you as you move forward.

1. **Eat three to five times a day.** Although it may take more preparation, Veggie Mamas agree that five meals a day instead of the common three help keep their children's energy balanced. Vegan foods are not as dense, so you will expect your kids to be naturally hungry more often. This is not a sign of malnutrition but rather a by-product of the clean-burning fuel they are expending. The best news is that children find a more natural balance of food this way, enjoying more healthy choices across each food group, due to the increased number of times they are eating throughout the day.

2. **Opt for whole foods over supplementation.** The American Medical Association suggests that children through adolescence should be getting their nourishment from whole foods rather than supplements. Taking in fiber and hydration through food ensures proper digestion by the body.

The only exception would be in the case of food sensitivities. I (Jenny) have found success supplementing my son, Dylan, who was born with numerous food allergies. I supplement with fresh-pressed green juice to deliver key nutrition without absorption issues. (Through the process of juicing, nutrients can be directly passed into the bloodstream without the need to digest the fibers first.) Smoothies are another "supplementing" technique, because the accompanying fresh fruits make superfoods and superplant ingredients like kale taste delicious.

That said, if you can choose whole foods as the primary base, making up 80 percent or higher of your children's nutrient intake, you will help develop a love of wholesome eating at a critical stage in development while at the same time ensuring their needs for fiber and hydration are met.

3. **Know that alkalizing foods matter.** Your daily routine dictates a lot when it comes to your child's balanced health, so build in alkalizing foods as part of that routine. What we mean is that although there are wonderful, numerous, and delicious recipes to vary your meals from day to day and week to week, make sure that at the core, you have some *basic* alkalizing foods. This could be the green smoothie we mentioned earlier, even as a side, along with another breakfast item. This alone can be powerfully balancing. Or you could incorporate a superfood like kale or spinach at least once every day specifically for its alkalizing effect.

Common Nutrition Challenges

As your kids grow and develop through the stages, you may run into specific health opportunities (the term we prefer over *challenges*). In this half of the chapter, we will be discussing how to best navigate through these situations as they arise. One important reminder before we begin our discussion: Be sure to stay calm and open. Most often solutions present themselves when you least expect them to. Patience and understanding, research, and optimism will support you in making incredible strides in your health journey with your family.

Here are some common nutritional challenges or opportunities shared by Veggie Mamas worldwide.

Food Allergies

As mentioned earlier, many children—and adults—are developing food allergies, intolerances, and sensitivities because of the modern toxic chemicals within the food (GMOs) or on top of them (conventionally sprayed pesticides).

- *Food allergies* occur when the body interprets a certain food as a harmful item and sends antibodies to fight against it. This causes symptoms ranging from rashes to anaphylactic shock, and can be fatal with even a small dose of the food allergen.

- *Food intolerances* are dose-dependent, meaning that you can eat a little of the food and not be affected. But when you eat too much, symptoms such as bloating, itching, runny nose, and stomach upset can occur.

- *Food sensitivities* are more difficult to pinpoint, because your body reacts inconsistently to the same food. One time, you might experience itching when eating it, and the next time you might have no symptoms.

A blood allergy test can reveal whether you or your family member has adverse reactions to particular foods. Avoiding these foods usually leads to a reduction or cessation of the symptoms.

If your child exhibits allergic symptoms, such as . . .

- Itching
- Sneezing
- Bloating
- Hyperactivity or difficulty focusing

. . . then it's a good idea to feed them the associated foods separately and monitor their reaction to each. Keep in mind, though, that symptoms can appear *a day after* the food is eaten. It can also have a cumulative effect, which shows up as symptoms long after the food was consumed.

Rashes

Skin rashes are a natural sign that a food allergy could be present, especially in breast-feeding babies. If your child is showing symptoms of eczema, for example, we recommend that you conduct a blood test to confirm the presence of any suspected food allergies. Children are also naturally sensitive to the world around them, and there are many potential toxins in the environment that could result in a rash. We encourage you to treat your child's rashes holistically, looking for the root cause, so that their immune system is best supported and they can find relief.

ALKALIZING VS.

CATEGORY	+4 MOST ALKALIZING	+3 MORE ALKALIZING	+2 ALKALIZING	+1 LEAST ALKALIZING
Herbs	Cloves, Cinnamon, Oregano, Basil, Turmeric, Parsley, Ginseng	Thyme, Cumin	Green Tea, Ginger, Peppermint, Spearmint, Marjoram	Curry, Sage, Licorice Root, Burdock Root
Fruits*	Avocados, Persimmons, Papayas, Lemons, Limes, Blueberries	Plums, Blackberries, Oranges, Tangelos, Mangos, Grapes with Seeds	Apples, Pears, Pineapple, Raspberries, Strawberries, Peaches, Kiwi	Apricots, Nectarines, Honeydew, Cantaloupe, Bananas, Currants, Cherries, Cooked Tomatoes, Watermelon
Vegetables* & Legumes	Spinach, Kale, Collards, Swiss Chard, Dark Greens, Broccoli, Arugula, Nori, Wakame, Kombu, Hijiki	Cucumbers, Zucchini, Parsnips, Green Leaf Lettuce, Romaine Lettuce, Brussels Sprouts, Bok Choy	Sweet Potatoes, Beets, Cauliflower, Carrots, Bell Peppers, Pumpkin, Squash, Garlic, Onions	Soybeans, Tofu, Jicama, Celery, Green Peas, Asparagus, Adzuki Beans, Black Beans, Kidney Beans, Green Beans, Hummus
Grains, Cereals, Grasses & Soups	Wheatgrass, Chlorella, Spirulina, Blue-Green Algae, Miso Soup		Oats, Sumac, Sorghum, Lentils	Quinoa, Millet, Amaranth
Sprouts, Nuts & Seeds	Sprouts		Almonds, Pistachios, Hazelnuts	
Oils		Cod-Liver Oil	Evening Primrose Oil, Borage Oil, Cold-Pressed Extra-Virgin Olive Oil, Flaxseed Oil	
Meat, Fowl, Wild Game & Shellfish				Perhaps Sushi, If Wild-Caught
Dairy & Alternative Milks		Breast Milk		Coconut Mylk, Rice Mylk, Soy Mylk
Beverages	Herbal Organic Teas, Bicarbonate	High-Quality Waters, Mineral Water		Filtered Water, Honey Wine, Red Wine
Sweeteners & Seasonings	Sea Salt		Blackstrap Molasses, Apple Cider Vinegar, Umeboshi, Stevia	

ACIDIFYING FOODS

CATEGORY	-1 LEAST ACIDIFYING	-2 ACIDIFYING	-3 MORE ACIDIFYING	-4 MOST ACIDIFYING
Herbs				
Fruits*		Cranberries, Raw Tomatoes	Canned Fruit, Shelf Juices with Sugar or Corn Syrup	All Nonorganic Fruit
Vegetables* & Legumes	Potatoes, String Beans, Chickpeas	White Beans, Navy Beans, Pinto Beans	Processed Soy Products	
Grains, Cereals, Grasses & Soups	Brown Rice, Kasha, Teff	Buckwheat, Wheat, Semolina, Farina, Spelt	Maize, Corn, Rye, Barley, White Rice	White Bread
Sprouts, Nuts & Seeds	Peanuts, Pine Nuts, Sunflower Seeds			
Oils	Sesame Oil, Grapeseed Oil, Sunflower Oil, Almond Oil, Peanut Oil			Fried Foods, Trans-Fatty Acids, Partially Hydrogenated Oils, Vegetable Shortening
Meat, Fowl, Wild Game & Shellfish	All Organic Free-Range Meat & Eggs, Pacific Wild-Caught Fish	Goat, Lamb, Goose, Turkey, Shrimp, Duck, Venison	Chicken, Beef, Eggs, Crab, Scallops	Pork, Oysters, Lobsters, Catfish, Atlantic/Farmed Fish
Dairy & Alternative Milks	Goat & Sheep's Milk Cheeses, Yogurt, Goat's Milk Products	Aged Cheeses, Organic Dairy Products		Cow's Milk, Cow's Milk Cheeses, Ice Cream
Beverages	Sake	Commercially Processed Black Tea		Soda, Diet Soda, Alcoholic Beverages
Sweeteners & Seasonings	Processed Honey, Raw Sugar, Brown Sugar	Vanilla Extract		NutraSweet, Equal, Sweet'N Low, Splenda, High-Fructose Corn Syrup

*Pesticides are acidic in nature, and fruits in particular, as well as other heavily sprayed crops like greens and root vegetables, will be affected by growing and spraying practices, making the food itself acidic. If buying conventional produce, be sure to soak and clean it well before consuming.

Following my own experience of dealing with an eczema skin reaction in my son, I (Jenny) have worked with many moms to find the root cause of the rash and then support the removal of the offending trigger. At one point, I was told by a trusted dermatologist that there was no recourse for my child's rash but that my three-month-old baby be given steroids. Luckily my instincts kicked in, and instead I opted for a blood panel to check for allergies. Sure enough, Dylan was allergic to seven of the eight potential allergens. Since he was only breast-feeding at the time, I was able to remove these foods from my own diet and his rash went away naturally, without the need for the medication.

This is a reminder that you will often be guided to look for alternative solutions for your child's health, and we recommend you follow these instincts in partnership with your child's pediatrician to find the most natural and effective way of supporting your family's best health.

Most Common Food Allergies

The following are the most common food allergies among children and adults, and some ways to adjust your meals to be nutritious and delicious without the allergens:

— **Milk and lactose.** Hands down, cow's milk is the most common food allergen for children, and in extreme cases, milk allergies are dangerous. Commercial milk is filled with toxic growth hormones and antibiotics fed to the cow, which are passed along to human consumers. Studies show that these additives can lead to acne in preteens and adolescents. Plus, compassionate consumers should know that the milk industry is very cruel to cows and their babies.

Fortunately, a plant-based diet is naturally dairy-free. There are many delicious substitutes for milk products, such as:

- *Nut mylks* made from almonds, sunflower seeds, or cashews.
- *Dairy-free yogurts* made from almond or rice mylk.
- *Hummus*, a wonderful substitute for melted cheese. There are also cheeselike spreads made from cashews.
- *Dairy-free breads* (look for the word *vegan* on the label).

— **Wheat and gluten.** Allergies to gluten are less common than sensitivities and intolerances. All three can create annoying symptoms, but to those with true celiac disease, the allergy to gluten is a health threat. Gluten is most commonly found in wheat—which, as we discussed, is often loaded with pesticides and other toxins. Organic brown rice is a wonderful substitute for gluten-containing grains, and these days you can buy rice bread, rice pizza crust, rice cereal, and other varieties.

With a raw, plant-based diet, you don't have to worry about gluten, because it's a naturally gluten-free way to eat. Unless you are making sprouted-wheat bread or using soy sauce, this statement should hold true. Even then, you could simply switch the wheat berries for buckwheat next time, and swap out the soy sauce for coconut aminos—these are the only two areas of concern with wheat on a raw vegan diet. Even wheatgrass juice is naturally gluten-free, since gluten comes from the wheat seeds, not from the green shoots, and the grass is cut above the seed for juicing.

— **Soy.** Soy and soy products (edamame, soy milk, soy yogurt, soy ice cream, soy butter, soybean oil, and so forth) are a leading allergen among children and adults. Many believe this is because the majority of soy plants are genetically modified, which means they have built-in chemicals such as *glyphosate* to instantly kill insects. Soy also increases the hormone levels of estrogen, which can be dangerous for those who have a family or personal history of breast-cancer issues.

Fortunately, there are healthful and delicious soy alternatives on a plant-based diet. We love homemade organic almond mylk (see the Merry Monkey recipe on page 88), for example, or faux cheese made from blended nuts.

— **Eggs.** On a raw, plant-based diet, you of course won't eat eggs. Compassionate consumers also avoid supporting the egg industry, which abuses chickens and chicks. Applesauce is a wonderful alternative to eggs for baking.

— **Peanuts and tree nuts.** Peanuts are a prevalent allergen along with tree nuts, like walnuts, almonds, Brazil nuts, pecans, and pine nuts. Nuts are a very common ingredient on a plant-based diet, so if symptoms appear, then a food-allergy blood test can confirm whether they are the culprit. Most people can safely eat seeds such as

flaxseeds, sunflower seeds, and pepitas as a nut substitute.

— **Fish and shellfish.** In addition to mercury contamination and the cruelty factor, fish and shellfish have become a common allergen for children and adults. On a plant-based diet, your energy needs will be fulfilled by high-protein vegetables such as kale, watercress, and broccoli.

Food Sensitivities and Intolerances

You or your child may not have formal allergies but still may suffer from allergic symptoms in response to certain foods because of sensitivities and intolerances. Common ingredients involved include wheat/gluten, sugar, additives, preservatives, food coloring, sulfates, and histamines. Since a plant-based diet is unprocessed, you won't have these food triggers in your meals, with the exception of histamine.

Histamines and Fermented Foods

Our bodies naturally produce histamine as a protective neurotransmitter whenever we ingest an allergen. Histamine causes us to bloat and itch, as a defense against toxins. In addition, when we're stressed, the hormone cortisol triggers the production of histamine.

Certain foods contain high amounts of histamine, and others trigger the release of the body's histamine. Some people are histamine intolerant, meaning that eating foods with histamine can incite allergic reactions. When we're stressed, we may develop an even greater sensitivity to foods that contain or release histamines.

Along with red wine and aged meats and cheeses, the most common histamine containers and releasers are:

- Vinegar
- Pickled and fermented foods
- Soy products
- Avocado
- Spinach
- Papaya
- Yeast

On a plant-based diet, you'll want to watch your child's and your own reactions to these foods. Histamine sensitivities usually yield immediate reactions of bloating, itching, heartburn, racing heart, or headaches, so they're easy to detect.

The alternative is avoiding these foods, reducing your stress levels, or taking an antihistamine to deal with allergic reactions. We don't recommend taking antihistamines unless absolutely necessary. It's much healthier to reduce your stress levels, or deal with stress in healthful ways such as yoga and meditation.

Addictions to Food Allergens

Ironically, we usually overconsume the foods and drinks that we have allergies and sensitivities to. In fact, so many of the foods we're allergic or sensitive to seem to be our *favorites*! This is because the binge reaction is an allergic reaction, in which the food sets off stress hormones that can temporarily feel like pleasure and excitement. In addition, overconsumption can *lead* to food allergies because of an unbalanced diet and the ingestion of too much of the same food type.

Abstinence from the offending food source is the usual prescription for dealing with allergies. Some people can slowly reintroduce these foods into their diets, while others have to abstain permanently. Allergy blood tests, working with a licensed nutritionist, and monitoring your own (or your child's) reactions to each food will guide your meal choices.

Anemia

Anemia is an iron deficiency in the blood and may show up as a child who easily bruises. This is important to watch for on a vegan diet, and there may not be immediate warning signs because iron stores diminish slowly over time in the body. Breast-feeding babies receive enough iron from mother's milk, but after the age of one when more solid foods are introduced, you'll want to be sure your toddler receives 11 mg a day. Adolescent boys need 11 mg, and adolescent girls need 15 mg once they begin menstruation, according to USDA nutrition guidelines.

Iron can be easily obtained in a plant-based diet through leafy greens, whole grains, tahini, and legumes. As a nutrition consultant, I (Jenny) have seen teenage children increase iron intake to ward against anemia by consuming hummus, made from garbanzo beans and tahini (both high in iron), and green smoothies.

Additionally, it would be good to ensure that your child is taking in 500 mg of vitamin D a day so that the body can better absorb the iron and build up the immune system. In an Oregon State University study published in 2009, scientists discovered that more than 50 percent of children and adults are deficient in vitamin D, and also demonstrated that an adequate level is an important function of immunity. Decreased vitamin D leads to chronic illness.

Diabetes

Childhood diabetes, spurred on by the rise in childhood obesity, is another issue that many kids and families are facing today. Symptoms of type 2 diabetes can be improved once processed sugars and flours are removed. Plant-based diets are highly effective for reversing diabetes symptoms naturally. Working with your endocrinologist or pediatrician is essential if you are facing this challenge in your home. With your commitment to a healthy diet and possibly the support of a trained nutritionist, your choices when it comes to what is at the end of your family's fork can play a pivotal role in addressing this condition.

♥

No one is as concerned about your child's overall health as you are! All the information reviewed in this chapter is a testament to the mothers and fathers who, over the years when faced with health opportunities like food allergies, have sought out answers for the sake of their children's well-being and fought for greater understanding and healing. The fact is, we are all unique, and our children are counting on us to learn and grow with them, looking for the best healthcare solutions. And balanced nutrition, of course, plays a central role. We encourage you to share this chapter's contents with other parents who may be looking for links to connect the dots for their children's best health. Hopefully together we can continue to make the future brighter for our families!

Chapter 3

Veggie Mama Fresh Cart, Pantry, and Kitchen Setup

What to purchase from week to week and where to find it is the focus of this chapter. There are certain categories of ingredients that you will be combining day in and day out in order to create nutritionally balanced, delicious meals, so we have outlined them here. Each foundational ingredient has been laid out, along with its key health benefits, so that you can zero in on those cart and pantry options best suited to crafting your family's personalized meal plans. (Remember that the shopping cart is where your Veggie Mama commitment begins—when in doubt, take it out!)

Routines for Life!

It's important to note here that at first getting your routine down for everything from shopping to preparation may feel overwhelming, if there's not as much support in your area. Once your habits become more stable and secure, though, everything will feel totally natural and you may even wonder why you didn't start this process sooner!

A point of encouragement here: Look online for local groups of Veggie Mamas who share information. Facebook has a variety of support pages where you can get to know other people embarking on the same lifestyle choice. We are all learning every day, and taking new things in; what's crucial to remember is that now you have done the research—you are well prepared. The new insights you gain here in your practical application of the Veggie Mama philosophy will be exactly what you need to be successful in your personal planning and wellness goals when it comes to key nutrition.

You should rest easy now and remind yourself to enjoy this process of learning with your children. Venturing into the kitchen together can help you all connect to one another and the world around you on a much deeper level. Building new routines, like shopping your local farmers' markets, can connect your family to more accessible and price-conscious products, as well as add to the spirit of adventure with food. Farmers' markets are an excellent place to try out new fruits and vegetables and sample different ingredients. If you have picky eaters in your family, taking them through the market with you and allowing them to experience new foods direct from the farmer can turn their food experience around!

Power Plants

In this section, we include some nutrition basics about the most beneficial common fruits, vegetables, nuts, grains, legumes, and seeds you can shop for each week. These really are plant medicines that will form the basis of health for your family. We were so curious to understand the great disease reversals brought about by adopting a plant-strong diet for so many people.

When you look at the potent properties of even the most basic ingredients that make up the shopping list for most of the recipes in this book, you begin to understand why this is such a powerful choice for the total well-being of the entire family.

Greens

Asparagus: As a superplant food, asparagus contains chromium, a trace mineral that allows the transport of glucose from the bloodstream into the cells, which is important for maintaining healthy blood-sugar balance. Asparagus is also a cancer-fighting superstar—rountinely consuming this vegetable reduces the risk for cancers of the larynx, colon, lung, bone, and breast. It can be juiced quite easily and added in with other fruits and vegetables as a powerful blood cleanser, which can be of big benefit during cold-and-flu season.

Broccoli: Broccoli is superrich in vitamin A, vitamin K, and B-complex vitamins, providing a great source of energy, especially in its raw state. It also offers very high levels of fiber (both soluble and insoluble), which can protect against bowel inflammation. Broccoli is an overall alkaline-forming anti-inflammatory vegetable and contains the bone-building minerals zinc, iron, magnesium, and calcium, along with protein.

Kale: Kale does not contain a very large amount of fat, but it is of the omega-3 variety called *alpha-linolenic acid*. Kale can lower cholesterol, and if eaten regularly, it can lead to a reduced risk of heart disease.

Kale is one of the nutrient-densest foods on the planet—beneficial for growing children, in particular. Kale yields 4 to 5 grams of protein per cup (equivalent to an egg) and contains a healthy dose of potassium and vitamins A, C, and K.

Napa cabbage: Napa cabbage is a great source of folate, an essential nutrient for DNA synthesis and important to consume during pregnancy and postpartum. Napa cabbage contains a good amount of *gluco-isolates*, organic compounds that fight cancer. For your children's health, just 100 grams of this cabbage will provide 45 percent of the daily intake need of vitamin C, and it also contains vitamin K.

Sea vegetables: Nori, wakame, kelp, and dulse are four staple sea vegetables commonly available. By providing a rich source of iron and B vitamins, sea vegetables fill important nutritional gaps that can crop up for growing children. Dulse is a great example—it's naturally salty and can be easily added to your next batch of guacamole to kick up the flavor—but a 1 teaspoon serving size will also supply protein, vitamins B_6 and B_{12}, iron, potassium, magnesium, calcium, and naturally occurring iodine, supporting thyroid function.

Spinach: Spinach is filled with flavonoids, which protect the body from free-radical damage from airborne toxins and toxins in food. Spinach also supports healthy neurological function by improving blood flow to the brain and decreases inflammation throughout the body. A cup of raw spinach has only 27 calories and is a great source of iron, making it a perfect nutrient-dense addition to smoothies and vegetable mixtures.

Zucchini: Zucchini is a well-balanced vegetable, which makes it an ideal selection for a wide variety of culinary applications. It's high in fiber, low in calories, and has a good amount of water content. Its peel is a rich source of dietary fiber, which helps reduce constipation and maintain system regularity.

Zucchini is abundant in potassium, supporting optimal function of the thyroid. It's high in vitamins C and A, as well as copper, and thus effective against asthma as a super-anti-inflammatory plant. We use it in the Veggie Mama kitchen as a base in soups to create body, in pasta to replace high-carbohydrate noodles, and as a staple for vegetable mixtures.

Herbs

Certain herbs can help protect against cancer, diabetes, and heart disease. *Polyphenols*, a class of plant compounds found in herbs and spices, are of great health benefit. Herbs can also prevent inflammation in the body. And green herbs, in particular, support the endothelial cells of the heart!

Basil: With more than 60 known varieties across the globe, basil is an important part of the Veggie Mama kitchen. It reduces inflammation and swelling with its array of vitamins and minerals, has antiaging properties (nice for Mom), and is rich in antioxidants. Basil varieties like cinnamon basil and opal basil have slight floral notes that are easy to pick out once you get used to working with them. This herb grows easily like a weed, even inside on the kitchen counter . . . the perfect place for little hands to help with harvesting. Planting basil is a simple exercise you can do as a family—and reap benefits from all year long.

Cilantro: Cilantro is a natural blood-cleansing agent. Chelating compounds in cilantro bind to toxins in the body, loosening them from the tissue. All herbs have very high antioxidant capacities, but cilantro in particular is a standout due to its vitamin K content, which supports the brain by protecting against the damage to neurons. And, with abundant potassium and iron, it is a nice dietary addition for building healthy skeletal structures as well. It truly is good for the body and the brain!

Green onions: Green onions are also superrich in vitamin K, vital to growth and development of bones, as well as protective of the brain. A rich source of folate for pregnant mothers and nursing babies, green onions have a powerful impact on the blood. The release of nitric oxide after they are consumed stimulates healthy blood flow and protects against blockages and clots. They are a mild onion, and for this reason we favor them in Veggie Mama recipes to appeal to kids of all ages.

Fresh Spices

The Veggie Mama philosophy makes use of several fresh and dried spices in order to create flavor, as well as enhance the nutritional qualities of each meal. Much like the green herbs mentioned in this chapter, fresh spices have a powerful effect, especially on the immune system.

Chiles: Chile pepper contains *capsaicin,* an alkaloid compound that makes chiles of all types effective for natural pain management. Many children do not enjoy spicy foods, but there are some who love them! In addition, small amounts of chile pepper may go unnoticed when balanced properly in a dish and will add a layer of flavor while also promoting overall health. Chile peppers contain potassium and vitamin E, so they support the healthy growth and maintenance of the skin.

Cinnamon: For thousands of years, this spice has been revered for its health benefits. There are really two types of cinnamon to be aware of: "True" cinnamon, or *Ceylon cinnamon,* has the most potent anti-inflammatory healing qualities, reducing blood-sugar levels and protecting the brain from plaque-building residues. *Cassia cinnamon,* found in most powdered cinnamon on store shelves today, is a relative of "true" cinnamon and offers similar health benefits, although not to the same extent. Cinnamon oil is a powerful fighter of fungal growth, and cinnamon cane is used to treat respiratory issues stemming from bacteria and fungi. As a culinary ingredient, cinnamon stimulates the digestive tract and helps as an antioxidant, creating balance in the body when consumed as part of your favorite desserts and savory dishes.

Garlic: Garlic contains an important compound called *allicin,* which high medicinal properties. Known for bolstering the immune system, it helps your body produce more of a protein called *ferroportin*, which increases your ability to absorb iron. Garlic can also aid in generating energy because it contains vitamins B_1 and B_6, as well as vitamin C, calcium, manganese, and copper. Garlic is easy to enjoy in sauces like pesto, but can also be juiced as a natural way to fight colds and ear infections.

Ginger: Ginger can easily be juiced or grated into numerous dishes and is naturally anti-inflammory. Ginger powers the digestive tract, and ginger tea can be effective for soothing an aching stomach. The *gingerols* compounds responsible for the root's spicy flavor have been found to be protective against the growth of cancer cells, and studies show they boost overall immune function.

Turmeric: Turmeric is a natural anti-inflammatory, matching the potency of anti-inflammatory medications. This herb in the ginger family dramatically increases the antioxidant capacity of the body, making it a powerful nutrient to prevent disease and create a balanced system. One active part of turmeric, *turmerone*, promotes repair to the stem cells of the brain, while another, *curcumin*, works to regulate blood sugar and protect against diabetes. Because of its anti-inflammatory qualities, turmeric can be effective in dealing with chronic joint pain. It can be juiced as a whole root or used dried in sauce preparations.

Colorful Vegetables

The more color the better when it comes to your family's dietary lifestyle! In fruits and vegetables, color itself denotes different vitamins and minerals. To keep an adequately balanced meal program going, you will want a full rainbow spectrum of fruits and vegetables.

Beets: Beets and their leaves are great ingredients in your weekly food preparations. Overall, both lower blood pressure, improve stamina, and fight inflammation. The beet itself is also a great source of folate and fiber, while the vitamin C content makes it ideal to include in juices to support immune-system function.

Carrots: A recent study out of the Netherlands found that fruits and vegetables with orange and yellow hues are significantly more impactful in preventing cardiovascular disease than those of other hues. The antioxidants and phytochemicals in carrots help with blood-sugar regulation, delay the effects of aging, and improve immune function. Vitamin A content is off the charts, and carrots deliver significant doses of biotin and vitamin K. This is one of the reasons carrots have been used as a first food for children for centuries. Naturally sweet, they offer nutritional benefits to a child moving into solids as a result of all the carotenoids in the plant, on top of its key vitamin and mineral provisions.

Eggplant: Eggplant is considered a brain food: The antioxidant *nasunin* in the skin is a protector of the fats in healthy brain cells, allowing them to properly regulate the excretion of waste. As a culinary ingredient, eggplant will take on the flavor of whatever you prepare it with, making it a very versatile ingredient that can also provide B_1,

B_6, folate, and vitamin K to support a healthy Veggie Mama and her family!

Mushrooms: With more than 100 varieties available for human consumption, mushrooms make an excellent substitute in the Veggie Mama kitchen for heavier, denser proteins. Mushrooms are as diverse as their names: Shiitake, cordyceps, reishi, cremini—it almost sounds like we are referring to a new collective of beings! Specific types confer different health benefits, but overall mushrooms have been widely known throughout the centuries to boost the immune system. Shiitakes, for example, are a good choice for supporting the digestive tract and building strength, while creminis offer a healthy dose of trace minerals. Dr. Joseph Mercola, a well-known integrative practitioner (mercola.com), as well as several other doctors who have studied the healing benefits of mushrooms, recommends buying organic mushrooms, as they are so strongly affected by their growing environment.

Red bell peppers: Bell peppers, or "sweet peppers," are actually all just different varieties of the same plant. In fact, green bell peppers are really red bell peppers before they are allowed to ripen on the vine. Sweet peppers (red, orange, and yellow) all contain beta-carotene and a large dose of vitamin C, more than your daily requirements in just one serving. We highly recommend enjoying red bell peppers raw, in particular, as many of their health benefits are lost to heat.

Sweet potatoes/yams: What's the difference between a sweet potato and a yam? Very good question! Sweet potatoes are the orange root vegetables that you have probably always identified as a "yam." True yams come from the Caribbean and are actually white with a yellow tint. Sweet potatoes have a large amount of fiber and, if eaten regularly, can help prevent heart disease and cancer. They contain 400 percent of an adolescent's daily need for vitamin A and make a fabulous base for many fun family dishes. As a bonus, yams have been found to be good for fertility, according to a study out of Harvard Medical School, by stimulating ovulation in women of menstrual age. The natural iron content also promotes lactation, so for pregnant and nursing Veggie Mamas, sweet potatoes/yams are a great cart grab!

Tomatoes: Tomatoes are most notable for their antioxidant-rich *lycopene* value, which makes them a powerful ingredient to support bone health. They are also abundant in biotin, which stimulates the production of healthy hair, skin, and nails. This is especially important during the postpartum period, when a mother is supporting an infant through breast-feeding as well as going through hormonal changes that shift the mineral content of her body. Beneficial lycopene, along with vitamin C, can be found in both cooked and raw tomatoes. However, studies have shown that the amount of vitamin C diminishes significantly in cooked tomatoes, while the level of lycopene increases. For this reason, it is a good idea to enjoy tomatoes in many different ways: as part of sauces, as well as cut and fresh as a topping!

Colorful Fruits

Fruits are known to powerfully cleanse the body, while vegetables provide building blocks for growth. You'll note that several of the colorful fruits we've chosen to include in this book are great for detoxifying the body and restoring balance on a daily basis.

Apples: "An apple a day keeps the doctor away" is a statement largely in reference to the *polyphenols*—the enzymes in apples that impart such an impactful health benefit. The enzyme that initiates oxidation, rapidly browning the apple once it's cut, is the same one that benefits our bodies. It's responsible for supporting the digestive tract for optimal health and vitality. Apples do seem to stand out as a powerful fruit, combating a wide range of health issues, from asthma to cancer.

Avocados: An avocado contains more potassium than a banana, has 4 grams of protein per serving, and delivers important healthy fats while at the same time lowering cholesterol. Some vitamins, like A, C, E, and K, need to be combined with fats, which act as a carrier for absorption. Thus, combining avocado with foods containing these nutrients will do the trick. A 2005 study in *The Journal of Nutrition* suggests that adding avocado or raw avocado oil to a salad, for example, increases the absorption of the other vitamins present at a rate of 26 times higher than normal. Avocado is also very satisfying and can make an excellent sauce and cream base that is free of common allergens and inflammatory ingredients.

Berries: Berries in general are a rich source of antioxidants and are low in sugar. All kinds are great options for integrating into juices and smoothies while still keeping the sugar content down. Blueberries stand out as an exceptional health benefactor because of their additional support of brain health. Termed *brain berries* by well-known "brain doc" Daniel Amen of the Amen Clinics, they have been shown to boost memory in many studies. In one University of Cincinnati study, participants who consumed blueberry juice scored much higher on memory tasks than those who were given a placebo. Other berries provide a full range of minerals to support healthy development and phytonutrients that aid in overall reduction of inflammation in the body. A study on strawberries demonstrated that their efficacy in reducing inflammation was increased by the regularity with which the participants ate them, so we recommend that you enjoy strawberries and other berries at least three times per week.

Grapefruit: Eating half a grapefruit per day will meet 64 percent of a child's vitamin C needs. In addition, the pectin in grapefruit juice helps clean the passageways to and from the heart. Grapefruit that are deep red in color are powerful for cardiovascular health and also rich in lycopene and choline. As a side benefit, grapefruit curbs hunger due to the enzymes it contains and can help stored fats exit the body. As your body shifts after welcoming a new life into the world, grapefruit can be a healthy addition to keep you fit and strong.

Lemons: Lemons are alkaline forming in the body, which means they can be powerful for reducing inflammation and supporting absorption of key nutrients. For this reason, we recommend using lemon juice instead of vinegars when creating your dressings and sauces. Lemons contain a significant amount of vitamin C, which helps the body produce collagen, aiding in a healthy complexion. These citrus, along with oranges, have been used to treat vitamin C deficiencies, like scurvy. Lemon juice is also a natural preservative, and sauces and spreads made with it will have a longer shelf life.

Mangoes: Mangoes are naturally sweet and almost appear to be nature's candy! Consuming these fruits can support optimal digestion, too, and because they are rich in minerals like copper, calcium, and iron, they are great for bone health. High in antioxidants, mangoes also help boost the immune system.

Melons: Melons are a very fun addition to any kitchen—they can be cut into shapes of all kinds, are widely varied, and, although still low in overall sugar, can impart a sweet flavor. Most melons are rich in potassium, while cantaloupe contains vitamins A and C and is a rich source of beta-carotene. Watermelon is perfect for a warm summer's day, and its high water content can help prevent heatstroke. At the same time, it delivers lycopene, the antioxidant that helps build healthy bones. Melons are high in electrolytes as well and stimulate optimal nervous system function. Melons paired with berries can provide a high-powered dose of antioxidants and energy. See the Cantaloupe Cups (page 74) for an execution of this idea.

Oranges: An orange has more than 170 different phytochemicals and more than 60 flavonoids, according to *Medical News Today*, and many of these natural chemicals have been shown to have anti-inflammatory properties and potent antioxidant effects. With a provision of more than 130 percent of a child's daily requirement for vitamin C, oranges of all types are good options to incorporate into your weekly routine when they are in season. Oranges should be juiced through a regular juicer, not a citrus juicer. Simply cut off the rind and leave the white pith intact so that the bioflavonoids can be absorbed into your juice to support healthy skin and brain function.

Pineapple: Bromelain is a special enzyme found in the core of the pineapple that aids optimal digestion. Pineapple can also be a great pick-me-up, as it contains vitamin B_1 (thiamine) and manganese, which help the body create energy. Pineapple is easy to work with and is an excellent base for smoothies and juices as well.

Nuts

Nuts may not be the right fit for every family, as some children are prone to nut allergies in their earlier years of life. However, once you know that nuts are not an issue for your own kids, we recommend integrating the following varieties, in particular, into your weekly food preparations as a way to readily provide essential fats and minerals. As a reminder, nuts and denser forms of protein should only make up 20 percent or less of a healthy, balanced meal program.

Almonds: Shopping for almonds means carefully examining the label. Look for almonds that are not pasteurized before bagging. These will have the highest enzyme value when sprouted or eaten raw. Almonds are a good source of magnesium, potassium, and vitamin E.

Cashews: Cashews should be used moderately, if at all, as they are the second-most-prevalent nut allergy, behind only peanuts. In fact, they are a relative of poison ivy! A symptom of an intolerance toward cashews would be swelling or bloating of the stomach. If you enjoy these nuts in your kitchen, be sure to get truly raw cashews that have been well cleaned, and sprout them prior to use. (See Chapter 10 regarding sprouting practices.) Between the shell and the nut is a "cashew balm" that is caustic to humans—and is often used as an insecticide! It must be carefully removed before the nut is fit for consumption. The good news is that cashews offer a wonderfully creamy texture, and they can be easily found in most parts of the world. They are also mineral rich—high in zinc, magnesium, and copper.

Macadamias: Macadamia nuts are an excellent source of energy production, delivering calcium, iron, and heart-protective selenium. A versatile staple for your kitchen, macadamias make a great nut meal and also cream up nicely in sauce recipes. The fats from these nuts are heart healthy and help lower bad cholesterol, which makes them a good choice for many

base recipes and an important ingredient for the health of the whole family.

Pecans: Although technically a fruit, pecans stack up high in terms of health benefits compared to other nuts, being rich in vitamins E and B, including folate. Pregnancy is a natural time to boost your diet by integrating pecans, with their health-giving content, and they also make a delicious fresh mylk—try them in the Mama's Mylk recipe (page 244)!

Pistachios: Pistachios contain the most protein as far as nuts go, delivering 6 grams per ounce. They are delicious in pesto—but, most important, they contain both calcium and iron! They are a standout Veggie Mama nut, for sure, because they offer so many of the life-giving essentials for vibrant health on a plant-strong diet.

Walnuts: A serving of walnuts contains 113 percent of the daily need for omega-3 fatty acids, making them an excellent choice for growing healthy brains and supporting optimal brain function. Ninety percent of the overall nutrient content of a walnut is attributed to its skin, so we recommend leaving the skins on for all the recipes in this book. Many moms note that adding walnuts—a rich source of biotin, magnesium, and copper—to their diets while nursing helps stimulate more production of breast milk.

Seeds

Seeds are less complex than nuts in structure and therefore are easier to digest. If possible, a balanced combination of fats from both nuts and seeds is recommended. However, if you are dealing with a nut allergy, you can substitute seeds at will for many of the recipes in this book (as well as the host of other books dedicated to plant-based lifestyles, as many plant-based chefs favor nuts). Seeds are much faster to sprout and contain more protein by volume than nuts. Here are our favorite varieties to work with:

Chia seeds: Chia seeds are a rich source of essential fatty acids, including omega-3, which supports brain health. Olympic runners report using chia seeds for optimal performance because the seeds provide condensed nutrition and can simply be added to water. We use chia seeds in the Veggie Mama kitchen to help hold recipe components together and to thicken yogurts, while at the same time providing important nutrition.

Flaxseeds: Flaxseeds can be found in both dark and golden varieties. The golden variety has a less pronounced flavor and can be a simple ingredient to create crackers and wraps with. Flaxseeds can be used as a thickening agent in a recipe, as well as to furnish a healthy source of dietary fiber and omega-3 fatty acids.

Pumpkin seeds: Pumpkin seeds, sometimes referred to by the Spanish name *pepitas*, are 20 percent protein by volume, yielding up to 27 grams per cup!

Sesame seeds: Sesame is a standout seed for three reasons: (1) It's incredibly high in copper, which helps produce collagen,

adding elasticity to skin, an important feature for pregnant moms. (2) It is high in calcium and iron, so sesame paste—tahini—is often used in this book to help load your diet with these two necessary minerals for moms and growing children. And finally, (3) it is a natural preservative due to the unique structure of its oil, so many of the sauces we create with it as a base feature a boosted shelf life, helping you spread out your time in the kitchen!

Sunflower seeds: Sunflower seeds are considered the best plant source of vitamin E; at the same time, they have twice the protein of either pecans or walnuts, with less fat and more fiber. Sunflower seeds make great bases for sauces and simple sprinkle-over toppings for many entrées.

Grains

In this book, grains will only be a minimal part of our food planning. Ancient grains, which have not been hybridized to improve crop retention, are typically higher in nutrient content and more easily absorbed by the body. Quinoa and buckwheat are great examples of gluten-free "grains" (these are both technically seeds, which makes them uniquely suitable for a grain-free diet).

Buckwheat: Buckwheat is an exceptional sprouted ingredient, and the raw milled flour is a great nut-free base in recipes. In diabetes studies, buckwheat has been shown to lower blood-glucose levels and insulin responses. It is also high in magnesium, which as a cofactor can contribute to the production of more than 300 additional enzymes.

Kamut: Kamut is the ancient relative of wheat and has been found in Egyptian tombs. Higher in protein content than wheat, it is easy to prepare and add to salads and soups in both sprouted and steamed preparations. Kamut provides powerful anti-inflammatory benefits and can play a role in heart health throughout life. A study in the *New England Journal of Medicine* reports that kamut is "much more effective" than modern wheat products in terms of its anti-inflammatory properties, as well as in antioxidant activity.

Quinoa: Quinoa, an ancient seed from Peru, is prized as a superfood. As a "complete protein," it contains all the necessary amino acids for total absorption and use by the body, and it's lower in carbohydrates than kamut and rye and is gluten-free. Quinoa can be prepared a number of different ways, making it an asset to any creative kitchen, and can also be a key source of protein for a week of Veggie Mama eating! It contains 8 grams of protein per serving, as well as more than 30 percent of the daily requirement of magnesium, so this pseudo-seed is great for Mom and baby!

Rice: Rice is also naturally gluten-free. Because this grain is higher in carbohydrates, we recommend you use it sparingly for your transitional recipes. Brown, red, purple, and black rice all contain more minerals than white rice, so we suggest you work with these more nutrient-dense varieties.

Rye: Rye is an excellent source of fiber, and compared to its relative, wheat, it yields about 80 percent more nutrition per bite. One benefit of the fiber from grains and sprouted grains has been reported by the Nurses' Health Study. Among the more than 69,000 women observed, those consuming the most dietary fiber from rye, in particular, had a 13 percent less chance of developing gallstones. Rye contains less gluten than wheat as well, and has not been hybridized in the growing process over the years, making it a possible alternative to wheat that is more easily digested by those with wheat sensitivity.

Legumes

Overall, legumes pack in some dense calories with little to no fat or cholesterol. Beans may not be the right choice for every family member, as those with sensitive digestion may develop gas or bloating, but particularly for very active members with a higher demand for calories, healthy preparations of legumes can be a part of a strong meal plan. Some great examples of simple recipes that incorporate legumes are our Hummus, Lentil Soup, and Sprouted Lentil Spread on pages 52, 123, and 204.

Garbanzo beans: Garbanzo beans are well known for their central use in the popular Mediterranean spread hummus. Chickpeas, as they are sometimes called, can be challenging for some sensitive bodies to digest without creating gas, so we recommend eating them sparingly. Used as a condiment, they can help boost the protein content of a meal and offer some great alternatives to high-carbohydrate snacks. In fact, in one study from the School of Human Life Sciences in Australia, scientists noted that participants felt more satiated and digestion improved when garbanzos were included on their plate. This is great news for any pregnant or nursing mama!

Lentils: Lentils are a rich source of dietary fiber and contain a wide variety of important nutrients: folate, iron, vitamin K, zinc, niacin, and more! We recommend lentils for your kitchen over other legumes because of their ability to be easily absorbed both as a sprout and cooked. Lentils should be used as a condiment or side rather than a main dish for best results and can be a great base for soups and even my (Jenny's) favorite gravy (see page 123)!

Peas: Peas have low but quality fat content, yielding omega-3 and omega-6 fatty acids. A great source of dietary fiber and protein, peas are also quite easy for the body to break down. Although they are often classified as a legume, they can be included in the "green foods" category that stimulates alkalinity in the body, and therefore helps in the prevention of diseases of all kinds. Peas also contain all the B vitamins, and for this reason, we use them as the base for our Energy Split-Pea Soup (page 127).

White beans: White beans, also known as navy beans, are a low-glycemic snack and actually help the bodies of sun-kissed children and adults repair skin oxidized by UV rays! For this reason, they are known as a "wrinkle-fighting" food, protecting collagen production, and are in the same category as the rest of the legumes in that they are high in protein and a great source of folate, iron, and magnesium. White beans are a nice addition to food preparations because of how soft they become even when sprouted, and their simple flavor makes them a good fit for children with sensitive palates.

Wholesome Sweeteners

Agave nectar: Agave is a succulent plant, and the sweetener derived from it is considered low-glycemic. Agave nectar can be found both raw and heat-treated. The rawer this sweetener, the fewer potential side effects involving the vital organs of the body. Heated agave has more fructose and could, in large quantity, create issues for the liver. However, raw extractions have less convertible fructose. For this reason, we recommend using agave nectar sparingly and a raw option wherever possible.

Coconut nectar: There are two types of coconut nectar: (1) technically raw coconut sap collected directly from the plant, and (2) a derivative of coconut by-products, low-heat-treated to create a sweetener. Both are low-glycemic sweeteners and have a rich flavor.

Dates: Dates are high in sugar, but if their fiber is kept intact as part of a recipe, they are a great choice for whole plant-foods lifestyles. With dates you also receive a healthy dose of minerals in every serving. Either process the dates down to a paste for easy integration in dessert recipes or use them whole as a snack on their own—they taste great stuffed with almond butter! Dates can be stored for an indefinite time period in the pantry or refrigerator, so you can feel comfortable buying them in bulk for your family.

Honey (raw): Raw honey, while only indirectly plant based (via nectar collected by bees), is a powerfully healing natural sweetener choice. It must be sourced from local and ethical beekeepers in order to ensure food safety for your family as well as the future of the bee population. If you are going to use this sweetener, be sure to buy it at a farmers' market or direct from a farm. You want to make certain it truly is raw honey, with all the beneficial enzymes and active probiotics. Used as a supplement, local honey is a great way to naturally treat seasonal allergies in children and adults. Raw honey is also beneficial in helping relieve and repair the digestive tract: 1 tablespoon with lemon in water per day would be considered a therapeutic dose.

Maple syrup (organic, grade B): Maple syrup is a mineral-rich, low-histamine sweetener, making it a good choice for allergy-prone family members. It is moderately high on the glycemic index, so it is not great for sugar-sensitive people—yet it is anti-inflammatory, so individuals with challenged digestion do well with desserts made with maple syrup. It is important to choose an all-natural grade B maple syrup to make sure there are no additives or coloring agents present.

Stevia: Stevia is technically an herb and does not spike the blood-insulin level at all because it is glucose-free. For anyone concerned about diabetes or other blood-sugar issues, stevia remains the best choice of sweetener. It comes as a liquid and a powder depending on your intended use.

Yacón syrup: Yacón is a root vegetable that can be harvested and low-heat-treated to produce a natural sweetener that is a prebiotic and also low on the glycemic index. Yacón has a natural maplelike taste and consistency, so it is a perfect culinary choice for desserts.

Basic Seasonings

Nutritional yeast: Both a seasoning and a supplement, nutritional yeast is a rich source of vitamin B_{12} and folic acid, important for pregnant and nursing mothers, as well as growing children. We recommend KAL brand, found in the supplement section of most health-food stores and online. Nutritional yeast—a nonactive yeast cultivated on molasses instead of a grain, as is traditional yeast used in baking—does not stimulate the growth of candida or contribute to other yeast-based issues in the body.

Sea salt: Sea salt is very alkalizing for the body because it hasn't been exposed to high heat like other table salts. Regular iodized salts are often stripped of their mineral content before packing and therefore don't offer any health benefits. Sea salt, however, is full of trace minerals—Himalayan pink salt (also technically sea salt), in particular, has at least 133—important for the blood and bones. In fact, you can help prevent osteoporosis by using sea salt because the bones are made of one-quarter salt! Sea salt also helps separate flavors in dishes so that you do not need to oversweeten or over-spice a dish.

Shopping Guidelines

As a veggie parent, you'll find that you are now mostly shopping the perimeter of the store, where fresh fruits and vegetables are kept, as well as the bulk aisle for essential base ingredients like seeds and grains. Where you find yourself in the store can lead to unexpected and welcome finds, as more and more healthy and clean products become available in the general marketplace.

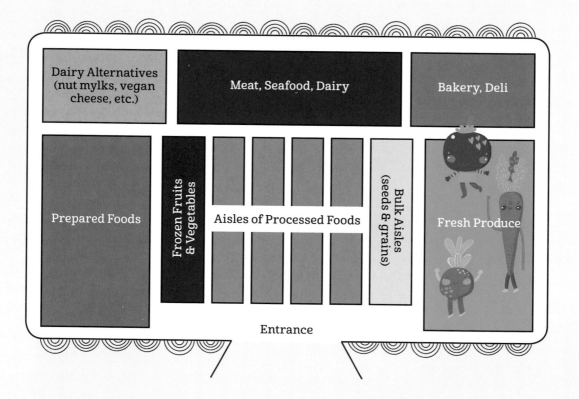

Dairy Alternatives (nut mylks, vegan cheese, etc.)

Meat, Seafood, Dairy

Bakery, Deli

Prepared Foods

Frozen Fruits & Vegetables

Aisles of Processed Foods

Bulk Aisles (seeds & grains)

Fresh Produce

Entrance

Veggie Mama Kitchen Setup

Simplicity is key for any parent, so this is a no-fuss approach to setting up your kitchen so that you can start with the basics and branch out in complexity as both your skill set and your passion for creating Veggie Mama cuisine evolves. Getting "back into the kitchen" can feel overwhelming, especially if you were raised in a fast-food family. Yet, food from your own kitchen can be just as quick, as long as you have a few staple tools and a stocked pantry. In fact, there are three main tools that will set you up for success in the Veggie Mama kitchen.

Veggie Mama Staple Tool #1: Blender

A good-quality, durable blender will go a long way toward creating just about everything in this book and beyond. A high-powered home blender like a dynaBLEND or Vitamix is preferred, as this is a tool you will use daily. The dynaBLEND even has a glass canister. All other high-powered blenders use plastic canisters, and there is a growing concern that plastics used in food preparation can negatively affect health. With every little step you can take to remove plastics and other chemically derived inorganic materials from your food supply, the better off you and your family will be.

Veggie Mama Staple Tool #2: Food Processor

Unlike your blender, your food processor needn't be high-powered or feature a large-horsepower motor. However, we recommended a food processor that has an 11-cup canister—or more, if possible—so that you can easily make double or triple batches of your favorite recipes! The S-blade attachment will help you create delicious hummus and other dips, while the slicing and shredding blades will cut down your prep time in the kitchen.

Veggie Mama Staple Tool #3: Mandoline

A mandoline is a simple tool used for creating different cuts of fruits and vegetables. On a mandoline, you can easily make zucchini noodles, or "zoodles," using the julienne setting, or long, flat noodles using yellow squash and the height setting with the flat blade. Sometimes just changing the cut of a vegetable can create a new texture that carries flavor differently.

Other Veggie Mama Basic Kitchen Tools

From here, the basics are all that's necessary to set up your kitchen:

Chef's knife: A 6- to 8-inch chef's knife will work for almost all kitchen needs involving fruits and vegetables. A Santoku blade is a nice addition to create even and clean cuts in fruits and vegetables with a high water content, while a paring knife will round out your set for more utilitarian projects, like coring and seeding red bell peppers. Ceramic blades, like Choisons knives, are a great option because they hold a sharp edge for a long period of time and help delay oxidation of the fruit or vegetable. This is especially apparent with fruits like apples; a ceramic blade will not brown, or oxidize, the site of the cut itself, and the food product will hold up longer once exposed to air.

Cutting board: You will be using your cutting board often, so we recommend a natural wood version to avoid introducing any toxins into your food from the board itself. A nice heavy and large board is a great choice for the whole family, especially since the less the board moves around, the safer it will be for your children.

Food dehydrator: As you progress in your culinary journey, you may wish to make even more fresh items in your kitchen using a food dehydrator. For raw-foods preparations, in particular, a dehydrator like the Sedona Express from Tribest is an important tool for your own wraps, breads, crackers, and granolas. Also, this tool helps minimize waste in your kitchen. For example, if you juice some carrots, you can then use the dehydrator to turn the solids into carrot crackers by creating a batter out of the pulp and other ingredients.

SALADS

SOUPS

JUICES

Glass bowls: Glass bowls for combining your fruit and vegetable mixes will be a welcome addition, and we recommend stocking your kitchen with at least three sizes in order to make different-scale projects even easier.

Glass storage containers: Glass storage containers will make all of your pre-prepped dishes look great in the refrigerator and keep them fresh for the whole week. Pick up a few different sizes so that it is easy to keep your refrigerator stocked and you have room for everything. For sauces and stored juices, Mason jars are great, as well, so that you can easily keep them airtight.

Juicer: For Veggie Mamas who love the idea of fresh juice, what is considered a slow juicer with a single or double auger will be a fun kitchen addition. Your kids can also get involved in making their next vitamin-rich

beverage so that they can feel the pride of "craftsmanship"!

Kids' fruit and vegetable knives: These are great tools for helping your kids get into the kitchen with you from a very young age. They are designed to cut through high-water fruits and vegetables but not pierce skin.

Salad spinner: If you have toddlers, they will gladly help you spin salad all day long! This also gets them into working with lettuces in a fun way!

Vegetable peeler: A Y vegetable peeler is the best kind for making carrot curls and other fun toppings and can easily be used by a child. As soon as children can hold this tool in their hand, they can be in the kitchen with you! This is an important step for kids to develop a love affair with fresh living foods and the culinary techniques for preparing them.

♥

Although we have included some important foundational knowledge in this chapter for setting up your kitchen for success, do not feel pressured to have this full setup to get started! All you need to get going with the recipes in this book is the motivation to try something new or broaden your current lifestyle, spicing it up with more variety and hopefully healthful add-ins that

support your family. As the world evolves, many more Veggie Mama ingredients and tools will arise, and your experimentation can continue. We recommend you always do a little research on new ingredients as they come on the market and stay connected to groups where healthy discussions are taking place so that you may be inspired by a like-minded community.

♥ ♥ ♥

Chapter 4

VEGGIE MAMA MEAL PLANNING

Veggie Mamas plan ahead to avoid food emergencies and to make sure they stay well nourished. A well-nourished mom leads to a well-nourished family! Planning doesn't have to include spreadsheets and scales, like in diet fads and other regimens. Planning is simply your pattern of shopping for, preparing, and storing foods each week, and cleaning as you go. If you wish to break the mold and step out as an adventurous Veggie Mama, you will have to bring more food preparation into your own home. For many moms, this pattern revolves around their work schedule, integrated with their kids' activities and the availability of a supportive spouse or other family members.

For the best results, we recommend that you begin by purchasing foods one or two times weekly, stocking up on all pantry items on the first trip and possibly just refilling fresh fruits and vegetables on trip two. On the shopping day or the day following, we recommend making your core recipes that can support a week of clean eating for the whole family. When at the grocery store, remember to shop the perimeter of the store, where the nutrient-densest foods, like fresh produce, are found. If you can fit in a trip to a local farmers' market, it may also help you stretch your shopping dollar because these fresh food selections also typically offer the best price direct from the farmer. For specialty items, like sprouted-rice tortillas and coconut flour, check your local health-food store.

Another word to the wise Veggie Mama: It may seem like food preparation is endless if you are dealing with diverse palates, multiple ages, and even food allergies. Don't feel alone in this! It is common to experience some natural stress as you adapt to the changing needs of your family. It's helpful to focus on one base recipe that works for everyone and then create different options for toppings or assorted sides that will allow you to meet the requirements for each individual in your family.

For example, a healthy pasta bar can include raw zucchini noodles, a bowl of cooked quinoa pasta noodles, and then two raw sauces, along with multiple toppings, which each family member can toss together and enjoy. To keep your sanity, make a few of these items during your prep days and then you can work from them throughout the week.

Here is a planning routine to support you when it comes to setting up your week for success. With this plan, we have also included a sample of three days' worth of menus and their corresponding simple recipes. (Raw-food dishes are marked with a *RAW* note.) As you become more confident, you can round out your meal options with more involved recipes in this book. This is a super-simple starter program that we have seen Veggie Mamas get great results with!

Suggested Preparation Schedule

✐ Sunday Evening ✐

— Shop for pantry items and fresh fruits and vegetables.

— Spend 1 to 2 hours making the following:

- 1 salad dressing
- 1 or 2 fresh sauces
- 1 dessert or snack dish
- 4 cups quinoa
- 2 sweet potatoes, baked

— Spend 1 hour cleaning and storing fresh vegetables. (For example, you may purchase celery and chop it down to hand-size sticks, or rinse off fresh grapes so they are clean and place them in a colander in the refrigerator for easy snacking.)

— Spend 20 minutes bagging up smoothie ingredients and store them in the refrigerator or freezer.

✐ Thursday Evening ✐

— Shop for additional fresh fruits or vegetables.

— Spend 1 hour rinsing and preparing vegetables.

— Spend 30 minutes to 1 hour preparing additional snack options for the next three or four days.

Here is how this plan works with simple recipes for a three-day period you can repeat later in the week if you'd like.

Veggie Mama Starter Meal Plan

Day 1

- Family 5 Smoothie (10 to 16 ounces per person in the family) **R**
- Hummus (4 ounces) and veggie sticks (1 cup per family member) **R**
- Zucchini Noodles with quinoa and Sweet Pesto
- Apples and raw almond butter **R**
- Sweet potato (½ per person), lightly steamed, with Sweet Cheese (2 ounces) and Veggie Mix or black beans (1 cup)

Day 2

- Family 5 Smoothie (12 to 16 ounces per person in the family) **R**
- Hummus (4 ounces) and veggie sticks (1 cup) **R**
- Quinoa (1 cup) with Veggie Mix (1 to 2 cups)
- Apples and raw almond butter
- Miso Soup with avocado, Zucchini Noodles, and Veggie Mix

Day 3

- Family 5 Smoothie (10 to 16 ounces per person in the family) **R**
- Hummus (4 ounces) and veggie sticks (1 cup) **R**
- Zucchini Noodles with quinoa, Veggie Mix, and Sweet Pesto
- Apples and raw almond butter **R**
- Sweet potato (½ per person), lightly steamed, with Sweet Cheese (2 ounces) and Veggie Mix or black beans (1 cup)

Veggie Mama Simple Starter Recipes

VEGGIE MIX

Double or triple the recipe to add this simple Veggie Mix into and on top of different dishes all week.

INGREDIENTS / INSTRUCTIONS

1 cup shredded carrot

1 cup chopped spinach

1 cup diced yellow squash or zucchini

Mix ingredients together in a bowl and then store in an airtight container until ready to use.

Makes 3 cups | RAW

ZUCCHINI NOODLES

Store these noodles separately from any sauces to prevent them from becoming too moist. When ready, simply toss with sauce and toppings.

INGREDIENTS / INSTRUCTIONS

4 medium to large zucchini

Julienne-cut the noodles on a mandoline or twirl them through a spiraling tool. Store them in an airtight container until ready to use.

Makes 4 to 6 cups, depending on the size and texture of the noodles | RAW

FAMILY 5 SMOOTHIE

Prepackage these ingredients in zip-top bags or reusable containers and store in the freezer until ready for use. You may wish to purchase frozen precut fruits, and we recommend choosing organic, if possible, to avoid the additives found in bags of conventional frozen fruits.

INGREDIENTS/ INSTRUCTIONS

2 cups chopped mango or pineapple

3 bananas

1½ cups kale or spinach

3 tablespoons hemp seeds or chia seeds

1 cup coconut water or juice

For 3 days of single 16-ounce smoothies, divide the ingredients evenly into 3 bags and store. Repeat this for each family member. It is better to bag these individually for easy "grab and blend," with no need to remeasure ingredients at the time of blending. Many moms report that time savings from day to day adds up! We highly recommend having your kids help you make these morning smoothie packs. When you are ready to blend, combine all the ingredients with ½ cup water or raw nut/seed mylk. Enjoy fresh, or pour into a mason jar or bottle to serve as an afternoon snack.

Makes three 16-ounce smoothies

RAW

HUMMUS

This recipe may be doubled and stored for up to 7 days in the refrigerator for use as a spread, dip, or replacement for dairy-based sauces.

INGREDIENTS/ INSTRUCTIONS

2 cups garbanzo beans (cooked)

⅓ cup lemon juice

2 tablespoons tahini paste

1 clove garlic

1 teaspoon sea salt

In a food processor with the S-blade attachment in place, process all ingredients until a thick hummus is formed. You may wish to add olives, sun-dried tomatoes, fresh green herbs, or curry, depending on the flavors enjoyed most by your family.

Makes 2 1/2 cups

RAW

SWEET CHEESE

This sauce is a great go-to paired with your Zucchini Noodles or inside of a wrap with your Veggie Mix. This cheese can also be easily converted to a dressing by adding extra lime or lemon juice and tossing with fresh greens. In addition, your family may like it as a dip for fresh cucumber!

INGREDIENTS/ INSTRUCTIONS

1 cup tahini paste or raw walnuts (soaked)

1 Roma tomato

½ cup water

⅓ cup lemon juice

2 tablespoons raw sweetener of choice

1 tablespoon nutritional yeast (optional; will yield more of a cheesy flavor)

1 clove garlic

1 teaspoon sea salt

Blend the ingredients well in a blender and refrigerate until ready to use.

Makes 2 cups

RAW

SWEET PESTO

This sauce will keep in your refrigerator for up to 2 weeks, so we recommend doubling the recipe! Use it on your Zucchini Noodles and toss in some of the Veggie Mix for a three-minute meal idea!

INGREDIENTS/ INSTRUCTIONS

½ cup extra-virgin olive oil

½ cup fresh basil leaves

2 tablespoons raw sweetener of choice

3 cloves garlic

1 teaspoon sea salt

1 cup raw walnuts, pistachios, cashews, or pine nuts

In a blender, combine the oil, basil, sweetener, garlic, and salt. Blend well until a green emulsion is formed. Then add in the nuts and blend again. If you have a nut allergy in your family, this recipe can also be made with soaked pumpkin seeds. For best results, soak the pumpkin seeds for 2 hours prior to use.

Makes 2 cups   RAW

AVOCADO LIME SAUCE

This sauce is simple to create and the best of all three sauces to use as a salad dressing or dipping sauce with fresh vegetables.

INGREDIENTS/ INSTRUCTIONS

1 avocado, peeled and pitted

½ cup coconut water

⅓ cup lime juice

1 tablespoon raw agave nectar or yacón syrup

1 teaspoon sea salt

Blend all the ingredients well on high speed until a rich, creamy sauce has formed. Refrigerate and use all week long.

Makes 2 1/2 cups   RAW

MISO SOUP

This is a simple recipe that makes a nice base for an easy soup any day of the week. While the soup itself is not raw, it employs lots of living enzymes by using the miso paste, and then adding in some raw vegetable components!

INGREDIENTS/ INSTRUCTIONS

4 cups hot water

2 tablespoons raw miso paste

2 tablespoons chopped green onions

Veggie Mix or Zucchini Noodles (page 49)

¼ avocado per person

½ cup chopped wakame (optional)

In a pot on the stove top, bring the water, miso paste, green onions, and veggies to a boil. Reduce the heat and pour into bowls for serving; top with the avocado and seaweed, if using.

Makes 2 1/2 cups | RAW

Important Reminder for Planning: Make Your Own Rules

Veggie Mamas know their routines best, so please feel free to use this basic guide as a springboard to create your own rules in the kitchen. The most important thing is that you commit some time each week to creating this opportunity for you and your family.

Scanning the simple preparation list and recipes, you can see how easy it is to shop for these basic ingredients and then simply blend, chop, and finally store these items for three days' worth of use. Mix up these recipes and make them your own, and add in your favorite ingredients to the bases—mushrooms to the pasta, for instance, and so forth. You can repeat this again after three days and then leave the seventh day for leftovers and dining out.

This part of the process is not about perfection but rather about finding calm in the middle of everything. For example, you may have a family member who does not enjoy hummus. No problem—simply switch this out for another protein-containing spread, like sunflower butter, tahini, or pesto. Later in the book, we include a chart of great options for brown-bag lunches for school to specifically address this area. It's important not to overthink the process of preparation but instead to be flexible and look for the opportunities to be creative about it.

We all have many life commitments and things out of our control that pop up throughout the week. So having a plan you can refer back to will help create some standards in your kitchen, providing a healthy food culture that will bring success.

♥ ♥ ♥

PART II

VEGGIE MAMA

Family-Friendly Recipes

Chapter 5

VEGGIE MAMA POWER-UP BREAKFASTS, JUICE SELECTIONS, AND SMOOTHIES

"The most important meal of the day" is indeed a critical one for getting in quality nutrients early on. *Breakfast* is so named because you are "breaking the fast" from the evening's rest and appropriation cycle. Your morning meal can be as creative as you'd like, as long as it delivers protein, essential fats, and a healthy dose of vitamins. The more alkaline and raw your breakfasts are, the better. You and your family are more likely to continue a pattern of healthy eating all day if you start off right!

Some Ross family favorites include Avocado Berry Breakfast Boats, Monkey Cereal and Mylk, and Cantaloupe Cups. These are great examples of raw breakfasts that are also well balanced.

Veggie Mama Rules for Setting Up Your Day

The key success factor for breakfast, as for any other meal, is creating balance. Traditionally, breakfasts are high in sugars and carbohydrates. The best thing you can do to turn this around is to think of first thing in the morning as "feeding the brain" time. After all, the brain will direct your activities for the remainder of the day. Coconut, avocado, flax, and chia are favorite whole-food fats and proteins from plant-based sources that stimulate the brain in the morning. Integrate these ingredients into existing breakfast menus to start out with, or make them the main attraction.

The recipes contained in this chapter are also easy to prepare in advance. If you make a large batch of Avocado Citrus Parfait (page 63) or Coconut Crème (page 67) on your preparation day, you can work from it all week to create delicious parfaits or to pair with fresh fruits. Our Mama's Magic Granola is positively divine and can also be batch-prepared to stock your pantry for two to three weeks at a time.

The other important key with breakfast is *not* to skip it! This may mean pulling out all the stops to prepare. If morning smoothies excite you, pre-bag the fruits to drop in the blender each day—then you can simply add a liquid and some superfoods to create a balanced meal on the run.

If you love the idea of the Strawberry Chia Crème, make four or five servings and store them in mason jars for a quick grab-and-go item. And the Grab-and-Go Breakfast Bars make perfect purse snacks and may be placed in the car or in your bag the night before so they're waiting for you when your kids are hungry or you are fatigued between activities and need a healthy pick-me-up!

Bowls of fruit can easily be added to a more transitional-style breakfast for extra enzymes, and cake stands with breakfast bars lined up help transfer the responsibility to your kids to pick out their own healthy breakfast. You may be more aesthetically focused, so an appealing presentation of menu items, like mason jars packed with parfait, is a sure way to create joy and abundance in your kitchen. Breakfast sets up the entire day for success, so make this a focal point and enjoy your own traditions that will emerge from putting good practices into place.

GRAB-AND-GO BREAKFAST BARS

For something to be grab-and-go in a Veggie Mama's mind, it must quite literally be "grab" and "go"! For best results with this recipe, we recommend packing the bars in fun bags with unique prints or small glass jars to facilitate the simple idea behind them. There are many options for flavoring the bars to suit your own family's tastes and nutritional needs. We've provided a few different add-in ideas as a jumping-off place to get your creativity going.

INGREDIENTS	INSTRUCTIONS
For the bar base: 1 cup raw almond or sunflower butter 1½ cups coconut flour or oat flour 3 tablespoons raw coconut nectar or raw agave nectar or 1 dropper liquid stevia 1 tablespoon ground cinnamon 1 teaspoon sea salt **Optional bar add-ins:** ¼ cup hemp seeds ¼ cup raw cacao ¼ cup carob ¼ cup coconut flakes 1 tablespoon orange zest	For the bar base, in a food processor with the S-blade attachment in place, process all the bar base ingredients until a thick ball or paste has formed. If using any of the optional ingredients for flavor or nutritional content, add them in now and process until well combined. Remove the dough and press into an 8 × 8-inch glass baking dish. Press down on top of the mixture with wax or parchment paper and roll over the mixture with a rolling pin until well packed. For easiest cutting, chill the bars for 20 minutes before serving. Cut into the desired size and wrap individually to prepare for easy grab-and-go selection. Be sure to solicit your family members for optional toppings that you can add to your breakfast buffet for their own versions of this bar. These bars are shelf-stable, so they do not need refrigerating; in fact, we recommend leaving them out for healthy snacking all day long!

Makes eight 2 x 2-inch bites or four 2 x 4-inch bars   RAW

AVOCADO BERRY BREAKFAST BOATS

This recipe is perfect for kids and adults alike because you can easily adjust the portion size for all ages and stages. The halved avocados look like boats, so this is also an especially fun presentation for families! This recipe can be made with either fresh or frozen fruits. Using frozen mixed fruits doubles as a nice chilled afternoon snack.

INGREDIENTS	INSTRUCTIONS
For the sauce: 1 cup fresh or frozen strawberries or mixed berries 1 tablespoon coconut oil 1 teaspoon raw sweetener of choice **For the boats:** 2 large Hass avocados 2 cups fresh or frozen mixed fruits	For the sauce, in a blender, blend all the sauce ingredients until well combined. (This sauce can be doubled for use as a garnish with numerous other recipes and makes a great substitute for syrup! It will keep for up to 7 days in the refrigerator.) For the boats, on a cutting board, first cut the avocados in half lengthwise and remove the pit. Then cut each avocado half lengthwise into 3 equal pieces. Place 1 to 3 portions on a plate for serving. Top with fresh or frozen fruit. Finish with the sauce garnish. Once complete, serve right away for that fresh-avocado look and taste.

Makes 6 to 10 servings | RAW

AVOCADO CITRUS PARFAIT

Avocado yogurt is a treat any time of the day, but especially in the morning. Avocado will stimulate the brain to get going—essential for performance in a school environment and for good cognitive function all day long.

INGREDIENTS

For the yogurt:

1 cup water or coconut water

⅓ cup raw coconut nectar or other natural liquid sweetener

2 tablespoons lemon juice

2 medium to large avocados, peeled and pitted

1 orange or 3 to 4 tangerines

1 teaspoon sea salt

Toppings:

2 cups diced orange or tangerine segments

1 cup diced strawberries

6 tablespoons coconut flakes (optional)

6 tablespoons hemp seeds (optional)

INSTRUCTIONS

For the yogurt, combine all the yogurt ingredients in a blender, loading in the liquids first. Blend on high for 30 to 40 seconds, until rich and creamy. Remove the yogurt and chill before serving.

For the toppings, prepare the fruit just before using in the parfait. After the yogurt is chilled, layer equal parts yogurt and diced fruit in a mason jar or parfait cup. Top the whole parfait with coconut flakes or hemp seeds, or both!

This recipe will keep for 4 or 5 days in the refrigerator.

Makes six 8-ounce servings

RAW

MAMA'S MAGIC GRANOLA

Veggie Mamas love granola! This is an anytime snack that can be served alone as a breakfast bowl, in a parfait, or as an afternoon-at-the-park snack. This granola *is* magic, because it is so simple to create and it is a crowd-pleaser every time! It can also be prepared in either the dehydrator or the oven. We love using the dehydrator for a high-energy, enzyme-rich combination. A low-temperature oven-baked version is still full of nutrient density—and of course made with the love of a mama and so better than any pre-boxed granola on the market!

INGREDIENTS	INSTRUCTIONS
For the granola:	If baking, preheat the oven to 350°F while mixing the granola.
10 cups sprouted* buckwheat	
1 cup coconut shreds	For the granola, in a large bowl, combine and toss together all the granola ingredients. If you need to add more sweetener or oil due to variations in the mix, pour in 1 teaspoon at a time until the mix appears well coated.
½ cup raw coconut nectar or raw agave nectar	
¼ cup raw coconut oil**	
¼ cup ground cinnamon	
1 tablespoon sea salt	
	For the add-ins, mix in any ingredients that sound like fun or deliver additional nutrition.
Optional add-ins:	
½ cup soaked raisins	Spread the mix no more than 1 inch thick either on dehydration trays that are covered to prevent leaking or on a baking sheet.
½ cup soaked pumpkin seeds	
½ cup sunflower seeds	
¼ cup soaked chia seeds	*For dehydrating:* Set the dehydrator at 118°F for 8 to 10 hours, rotating the granola halfway through to change the drying surface
2 tablespoons orange zest	
	For baking: Place the granola in the oven for 25 minutes, tossing halfway through.

*Sprouting buckwheat is painless and simple, and we recommend involving your children in this process as well. This is a great visual to show the living aspect of foods they are enjoying. Simply place the buckwheat in a clear glass bowl three times the volume of the dry groats. Cover with water by 2 inches above the line of the groats. Soak for 8 to 12 hours and then rinse prior to using. You will notice the groats are both soft and have a small tail coming off the point of the grain.

**Raw coconut oil is semisolid at room temperature or slightly warm. It may help to massage this oil into the blend to help further liquefy it if it becomes stubbornly solid.

Makes 16 cups, plus add-ins   RAW or TRANSITIONAL

COCONUT CRÈME

·•✦•·

Coconuts are an incredible source of healthy fatty acids. This crème is more on the sweet side than the Avocado Citrus Yogurt featured in the parfait (page 63). For this reason, it can also double as a dessert! Simply mix with fresh fruit for a seasonal parfait. In this breakfast recipe presentation, we recommend pairing it with papaya or pineapple due to the additional enzymes that aid digestion, or blueberries to boost the antioxidant content.

INGREDIENTS

For the coconut crème:

1½ cups water or coconut water

⅓ cup raw sweetener of choice

6 cups young Thai coconut flesh

1 teaspoon sea salt

For the topping:

1 cup diced pineapple

1 cup diced papaya

1 cup blueberries

Juice of 1 lime (optional)

INSTRUCTIONS

For the coconut crème, in a blender, combine all the ingredients, loading in liquids first. Blend on high speed for 30 to 40 seconds, until well combined and rich and creamy. Some coconuts are naturally thicker than others—this is the unique aspect of Mother Nature (the original Veggie Mama!). You may need to add more moisture to thin out the mix to a creamy texture, adding 2 tablespoons of water at a time, until you reach the desired consistency.

Chill the crème until ready to enjoy.

For the topping, toss all the fruit together in a medium mixing bowl. Drizzle the lime juice over the fruit.

When ready to enjoy, combine the crème and the fruit in ramekin bowls or other fun serving dishes.

This is a great make-ahead recipe, and the fruit and crème can easily be kept separate and combined at the time of serving for a week's worth of breakfasts.

Makes 8 cups (Recipe may be halved for great results as well.) | RAW

STRAWBERRY CHIA CRÈME

Chia seeds and banana make a great base for this healthy crème that is easy to prepare and then enjoy all week long. This recipe calls for strawberries, but mixed berries are a great substitute, as well as watermelon! Make this crème your own by experimenting with other fruits that your kids love.

INGREDIENTS

For the strawberry crème:

1½ cups water or coconut water

4 bananas

2 cups strawberries

¼ cup white chia seeds

1 dropper stevia

Optional add-ins:

¼ cup coconut oil or coconut butter

¼ cup coconut flakes

INSTRUCTIONS

For the crème, combine all the ingredients in a blender, loading in the liquid first and adding any of the optional add-ins. Blend well. This quick blend should be a snap!

Transfer the mixture to easy refrigerator containers, like mason jars. This crème will get thicker as it sits and will eventually become almost like a thick porridge.

This recipe should be enjoyed within 5 days of preparation for best results and is lovely topped with dried fruits, nuts, seeds, and superfoods of all types.

Makes six 8-ounce servings | RAW

BREAKFAST BURRITO, FAMILY-STYLE

We prepare these burritos as a group in the Ross household. We take the base mixture and then we each add our own favorite items to make them uniquely suited to our tastes, wrap, roll, and serve. If you have a large tribe, you can also make these burritos in batches and save them for serving in an hour or two if you have a morning itinerary to manage.

INGREDIENTS

For the sauce:

1 cup tahini paste

½ cup diced tomatoes

¼ cup lemon juice

1 tablespoon light chile powder

1 clove garlic

1 teaspoon sea salt

1 teaspoon raw sweetener of choice

½ cup water

For the filling:

1 cup shredded carrot

1 cup shredded zucchini

1 cup chopped spinach

½ cup diced tomatoes

½ cup diced mushrooms

½ cup diced mango or pineapple

½ cup diced avocado

½ cup walnut pieces (optional)

INSTRUCTIONS

**For the wrap
(choose the best option for you):**

6 Easy Wraps (page 146);

6 brown-rice tortillas; or

6 collard green leaves (stems removed)

For the sauce, blend all the sauce ingredients until well combined. Transfer the sauce to an easy storage container, and if preparing in advance, refrigerate until ready to use. If using immediately, leave out at room temperature for best flavor.

For the filling, in a medium mixing bowl, combine all the filling ingredients and top with the sauce. Toss until well coated.

Fill each wrap evenly, and serve them right away.

Makes 6 burritos

MONKEY CEREAL AND MYLK

·⊹·

Cereal took on a whole new meaning when this Veggie Mama (Jenny) began trying to help my family enjoy cereals that were not covered in sugars and packed full of carbohydrates. This is a simple mix that my veggie kids love and does not require any baking or dehydrating! It's simple enough that the younger ones can prepare it themselves yet still interesting enough that it holds their attention.

INGREDIENTS	INSTRUCTIONS
For the cereal:	For the cereal, after all the grains have sprouted for 12 hours, rinse them well and toss together in a bowl. Add the remaining cereal ingredients.
2 cups sprouted buckwheat groats*	
1 cup sprouted white quinoa*	
1 cup sunflower seeds	For the mylk, in a blender, blend all the mylk ingredients on high speed until well combined.
1 cup pumpkin seeds	
½ cup golden mulberries (dried)	*Simply place the buckwheat and quinoa in clear glass bowls three times the volume of the dry seeds. Cover with water 2 inches above the line of the seeds. Soak for 12 hours and then rinse prior to using. You will notice the buckwheat groats and quinoa are both soft and have a small tail coming off the point of the seed.
½ cup almonds or pecan pieces	
¼ cup chia seeds	
For the mylk:	
1 cup pecan or walnut pieces	
4 cups water	
1 pinch sea salt	
1 teaspoon vanilla paste or powder (optional)	

Makes six 1-cup servings

RAW

PUMPKIN FLAX WAFFLES

Transitional recipes like this one offer a healthy breakfast treat, and you can rest easy because you know the ingredients are all whole foods. Even though we are cooking them, creating a more dense meal option, this can be balanced by adding in fresh fruit and vegetable dishes throughout the day. You can feel great about this recipe that adds a healthy dose of omegas to a morning meal and features a natural sweetener that will not overstimulate your family and upset blood-sugar balance. You will need a waffle iron or plug-in waffle maker to make this breakfast dish.

INGREDIENTS	INSTRUCTIONS
1 cup gluten-free oat flour	Preheat a waffle iron to the medium setting while preparing the waffle mixture.
1½ cups all-purpose gluten-free flour mix	
1 teaspoon baking powder	In a medium mixing bowl, combine the flours, baking powder, baking soda, salt, cinnamon, and flaxseeds. In another mixing bowl, combine the mylk, oil, pumpkin puree, and sweetener and blend using an immersion blender. (A basic blender may also be used in place of the immersion blender.)
1 teaspoon baking soda	
1 teaspoon sea salt	
2 tablespoons ground cinnamon	
2 tablespoons ground golden flaxseeds	
1 cup almond mylk	
2 tablespoons coconut oil	Pour the liquid mixture over the dry mixture and whisk together until you have a silky batter to work with. Then lightly coat the waffle iron with olive oil. Take ½ to ¾ cup of the mixture, depending on the size and shape of your waffle maker, and coat the bottom portion lightly with batter. Close the waffle iron. When the steam diminishes from the sides, check to see if the waffle is ready. It should be crispy and light.
8 ounces pumpkin puree (canned or fresh)	
⅓ cup raw agave nectar, honey, or maple syrup (save additional amount if you wish to use the same sweetener as a garnish)	
Olive oil, for coating waffle iron	
Toppings:	Keep the waffles in a warm oven until ready to serve. Top with fresh fruit, nut butter, or the natural sweetener of your choice.
2 to 4 tablespoons nut butter of choice	
2 cups fresh fruit	

Makes 8 waffles

CANTALOUPE CUPS

Melons are very high in electrolytes and represent their own subcategory of fruits. Some folks with sensitive digestion find melons hard to digest with other categories of fruits. For this reason, we recommend you enjoy them alone or with berries for best digestive results. These Cantaloupe Cups combine three varieties of easy-to-find melons that are also very colorful and pleasing to the eye. Melons make a nice morning snack and can help alkalize the body, reducing inflammation. This can be a great go-to solution for swollen ankles during pregnancy and for healing from common colds and flus for veggie kids!

INGREDIENTS	INSTRUCTIONS
Four 1-inch-thick watermelon slices 2 cups diced honeydew 2 cups diced cantaloupe ¼ cup fresh mint leaves, for garnish (optional)	Using a cookie cutter of your choice, cut a shape out of each watermelon slice. Set the watermelon cutouts aside. Lay the watermelon slices on a plate for individual servings. In a medium bowl, toss the honeydew and cantaloupe pieces together and fill each watermelon slice with 1 cup of the fruit. Then, in a blender, blend the watermelon cutouts. Serve the watermelon juice alongside the plate or drizzle over the other melon pieces for added flavor. Garnish with the mint leaves for added flavor and color.

Makes 4 cups

RAW

Power-Up Juice Selections

Juicing is a simple way to add more essential vitamins and minerals to your family's lifestyle. Think of juices as a concentrated shot of the good stuff. These recipes, in particular, balance sugars with bone-building greens and root vegetables to create simple blends the whole family will love. Consider adding in some of the functional superfoods, too, to get in important categories of nutrients that may otherwise be hard to translate to your youngest family members.

For instance, I (Jenny) love to add coconut oil to Dylan's green juice. He doesn't particularly enjoy the coconut on its own, but he does when it's mixed into the juice—and he benefits from the ready absorption into his happy, healthy body! Juices deliver nutrients without fibers, so instead of gradual processing through the digestive tract, they are carried quickly into the bloodstream. For this reason, in particular, you want to steer clear of pasteurized juices that are high in sugars with the fibers removed, and when juicing at home with your family, be sure to create blends that are a nice combination of low-sugar fruits and vegetables. Pasteurized juices have three to four times the sugar content of cold-press or fresh-pressed juices, because the sugar content is increased as the juice is exposed to heat. When this high-sugar juice quickly enters your bloodstream, it artificially spikes blood-sugar levels and creates an imbalance in the body.

When done right, juicing can be a powerful way to help support your child's body, especially during cold-and-flu season, by readily delivering some extra nutrients. When you are using these cold-pressed juice options, or even fresh-pressed, unpasteurized juices, you are supporting the immune system with additional enzymes, vitamins, and minerals. Since there is no heating involved in this process, make sure you wash and clean your fruits and vegetables well before juicing to eliminate any harmful bacteria and pesticides.

♥

Juicing tip: Juices are best prepared fresh or in a cold, slow juicer. If you work with a centrifugal juicer, enjoying it the same day it is prepared maximizes the nutritional benefit. Cold-press juicers, like the Green Star, can be used to pre-prep juice up to 3 days in advance.

Juicing steps: Combine one or two juice bases, preferably one sweet and one salty, with additional nutrients to make your own personal blends.

JUICE BASES (¼ to ½ cup)	NUTRIENT-DENSE FRUIT AND VEGETABLES (combine to create ½ cup)	SUPERFOODS TO ADD IN AFTER JUICING (add single-serving portion after juice is complete)
Cucumber (SALTY)	Spinach/romaine/kale	Hemp seeds
Celery (SALTY)	Beets, purple and gold	Vegan protein powder
Pear (SWEET)	Dandelion greens/kale/ collard greens	Maca root (for adults only—regulates hormones)
Zucchini (SALTY)	Ginger/turmeric	Coconut oil

All juice recipes are for single-serving portions yielding 12 to 16 ounces of juice, depending on the unique fruits and vegetables used.

DOREEN'S GREEN BLEND

2 apples

2 cups spinach

1 teaspoon spirulina

1 inch ginger root (optional)

ORANGE TURMERIC

1 orange, peeled

1 cup pineapple chunks

1 carrot

1 inch turmeric root or
1 teaspoon turmeric powder

EASY GREENS

2 cups pineapple chunks

2 cups kale

2 stalks celery

1 cup spinach

VEGGIEPALOOZA

2 carrots

1 cup chopped beets

4 stalks celery

1 cup spinach

½ lemon, peeled

CUCUMBER MINT

2 cups chopped cucumber

½ apple

1 cup kale or spinach

1 sprig mint

PINK LEMONADE

1 lemon, peeled

1 apple

1 cup strawberries

1 inch ginger (optional)

TERRIFIC TOMATO

2 Roma tomatoes

2 stalks celery

1 cup chopped cucumber

1 cup chopped apple

½ lemon, peeled

WATERMELON LEMONADE

(MAY BE BLENDED OR JUICED WITH GREAT RESULTS)

2 cups chopped watermelon

½ lemon, peeled

Smoothies

Delivering a different type of food nourishment than juices, smoothies still contain a healthy amount of fiber. For this reason, then, they can be considered a "meal in a cup" as long as they contain all the key nutrients for a balanced meal. It's the same way we would apply the basic tools for nourishment when working with entrées and salads, for example. Smoothies, because you can blend in all kinds of nutrients, are also a super place to get essential supplements like probiotics into a meal for kids of all ages. If you have a great base of fresh seasonal fruits, you can blend in greens, oils, and other hard-to-integrate nutrient categories and still come out with a sweet and fruity beverage both kids and adults will love.

Depending on the age and stage of your child, you will want to serve 6 to 16 ounces. Growing teenagers would enjoy an adult-size serving of 16 ounces, whereas toddlers do best with their smoothie in a sippy cup with a straw so they can "graze" on it all morning or afternoon. We recommend starting with 6 ounces and working your way up as your toddler ages. These are our favorite smoothie blends and some of the inherent health benefits of each; they are a great start for your own recipe collection.

Veggie Mama Idea for the Adventurous Family: Smoothie Bar

Kids love to make their own smoothies, and it's a great way to get young minds and hearts moving in the kitchen, working with fresh fruits and vegetables. Creating a smoothie bar that kids can make their own selections from and offering different "add-ins" will make this a welcomed routine. A great tool for keeping this organized and easy is to get a NutriBullet or personal blender with multiple tops so that each member of the family can load the top with his or her own favorites, blend, sip, and enjoy! You can also do this in advance and come back to the smoothie within 4 to 6 hours for an afternoon snack. One easy way for your kids to help out if smoothies will become a morning routine is to pre-bag the smoothie ingredients and place them all in the freezer. You can include in the bag everything that is going in the blender, save the liquid. This way all that has to happen in your busy morning routine is to drop it in, add liquid, and blend!

MAMA'S MORNING SMOOTHIE

Mama needs hearty nutrition, and it can sometimes present a challenge to get in a balanced meal while providing for the needs of a growing family. This smoothie is designed to boost a Veggie Mama's energy naturally and effectively so you can keep your tribe moving. One option is to make this smoothie without ice, place it in an easy-to-grab blender bottle, and shake it up throughout the day for "self-nurturing" on the run.

INGREDIENTS	INSTRUCTIONS
1 banana	Blend all the ingredients in a high-powered blender until well combined.
1 cup fresh or frozen berries	
½ cup spinach	Transfer to a serving cup or blender bottle for later use.
⅓ cup raw vegan vanilla protein mix (try whole pea protein as a great option in this smoothie)	*Maca root should not be used in preparations intended for children because it stimulates hormone production. If you are sharing this smoothie with the whole family, it's best to leave it out.
1 tablespoon raw coconut oil or hemp seeds	
1 tablespoon spirulina or greens powder mix	
½ cup water or almond mylk	
1 cup ice	
1 tablespoon maca root (optional*)	

Makes one 16-ounce serving

RAW

SUPERGREEN GOODNESS

The supergreen smoothie is a wonderful tool to help kids of all ages get comfortable with the color green! Those who may not be familiar with the taste of spinach, kale, or other deep green vegetables may be intimidated by the dark color. Getting over this hurdle can be simple if you keep it fun. Children are sensitive to the look of their food, and if they are apprehensive about green, this smoothie recipe may help you move through this. The great news is that the tropical fruits help balance the bitterness in the greens, imparting a nice sweet flavor that allows kids the opportunity to, perhaps, look at them in a new light. This is an excellent place to add some extra proteins and mineral-rich superfoods like spirulina to their diet.

INGREDIENTS	INSTRUCTIONS
½ to ¾ cup coconut water (regular water may substitute)	Add the liquid to the blender followed by all the fruits and vegetables as well as the superfoods. Blend until well combined.
1 cup chopped mango or pineapple (frozen is best for a frothy smoothie)	This recipe works great in all blenders. For the best taste and texture, you may add a little extra blending time for blenders that are not high powered so that all the leaves are well combined with the fruits.
1 banana	
½ to 1 cup spinach or kale, stems removed*	
1 tablespoon spirulina or supergreens powder by Dr. Schulze or Vital Greens	*The amount of greens you use per smoothie will depend on your child's flavor sensitivity. If you are starting kids off early with green smoothies, we recommend you go ahead and use a whole cup. For kids who are new to green smoothies and may be trepidatious, start with ½ cup, and as their tastes evolve, work your way up to a whole cup. The difference is slight, but some children are more sensitive than others to the flavor of fresh leafy greens.

Makes one 16-ounce serving   RAW

CHOCOLATE SUPREME

This smoothie lets your kids indulge in a healthier form of chocolate. Chocolate still is a natural stimulant, so you want to use it in a balanced way. You can think of this smoothie as a great source of nutrition that might take the place of the more "treat"-type foods they have enjoyed in the past. This works especially well for teenagers.

INGREDIENTS	INSTRUCTIONS
1 banana	Add all the ingredients to the blender. Include ice for a creamier smoothie, or leave it out for more of a rich chocolate mylk.
¼ cup raw cacao	
1 tablespoon raw agave nectar, coconut nectar, or stevia	
1 cup nut or seed mylk	Blend on high speed for approximately 30 seconds.
1 teaspoon ground cinnamon	Pour into a cup and enjoy!
1 tablespoon raw nut or seed butter	
1 tablespoon hemp seeds	

Makes one 16-ounce serving   RAW

MANGO MADNESS

Mango is a flavor beloved by kids, and the fruit creams up nicely in smoothies as well as Popsicle mixtures. In fact, this smoothie blend can be poured into Popsicle trays to freeze for a functional treat in the summer months. Its vibrant color is a welcome surprise! The berry puree is an option for making this smoothie stand out as eye candy as well. It's true that we eat with our eyes first, so this is also a great beginner recipe for plant-based lifestyles.

INGREDIENTS	INSTRUCTIONS
For the berry puree: 1 cup fresh or frozen berries ¼ cup water **For the smoothie:** 1 cup chopped mango (frozen or fresh; if fresh, add 1 cup ice) 1 banana ¾ cup orange juice 1 tablespoon coconut oil or butter 1 teaspoon hemp or chia seeds (optional)	For the puree, in a blender, blend all the berry puree ingredients until well combined. I (Jenny) like to use my smaller personal blender for this recipe because the volume of liquid is less than 16 ounces. Transfer the mixture to a squeeze bottle and then refrigerate before use. For the smoothie, in a basic blender, combine all the smoothie ingredients and blend on high speed until well combined. To serve, squeeze the berry puree around a clear cup, and then fill with the smoothie. If making these into Popsicles, first pour in 1 ounce berry puree, followed by 6 ounces smoothie, followed by another 2 ounces puree.

Makes one 16-ounce serving | RAW

BERRY BLAST-OFF

Berries are very high in antioxidants and represent a perfect source of nutrition during the early fall, especially, to boost the immune system. This smoothie is also low in sugar, as berries are a low-glycemic fruit. The added coconut in this smoothie makes it a good choice for boosting brainpower, and if you choose blueberries, you will multiply the benefit.

INGREDIENTS	INSTRUCTIONS
1 cup fresh or frozen berries (choose a berry mix for a smoothie that is less tart)	Blend all the ingredients on high speed until well combined.
1 banana or ½ avocado (avocado is best for sugar-sensitive family members)	Enjoy right away!
1 cup coconut water	
2 tablespoons coconut shreds	
2 tablespoons hemp seeds	

Makes one 16-ounce serving | RAW

MERRY MONKEY

Monkeys are very strong and smart animals—and live well on a plant-based diet—just like us! Their meals consist mostly of fruits and nuts, with some leafy greens. This smoothie is affectionately named after the banana-loving monkeys depicted in children's stories. We've combined the fun and the functional here—enjoy this smoothie as a beneficial introduction to how delicious plant-based foods can be!

INGREDIENTS	INSTRUCTIONS
1½ bananas 1 cup Quick Almond Mylk* 2 tablespoons raw nut or seed butter 1 teaspoon ground cinnamon 1 teaspoon vanilla paste (optional) 1 teaspoon raw agave nectar or 2 drops stevia 1 cup ice	Blend all the ingredients on high speed until well combined. Add optional toppings, like the Cacao Sauce (page 182) for a mylk-shake experience, or the Berry Puree (page 182).

Makes one 16-ounce serving	RAW

*QUICK ALMOND MYLK

INGREDIENTS	INSTRUCTIONS
1 cup soaked raw almonds (soak for 12 hours and rinse prior to use) 3 cups water 1 teaspoon vanilla paste or powder 1 pinch sea salt	Blend all ingredients well in a high-powered blender for best results. Strain using a colander or cheesecloth. Refrigerate and store for up to 5 days.

Makes 4 cups	RAW

GORILLA GREENS

No one asks a gorilla whether it gets adequate protein—it's a given from the large, commanding stature of this veggie-loving primate! In this smoothie, you will be getting more than 20 grams of protein from the greens and nuts. This is a powerful way to support growing teenagers with additional calorie needs, without loading them up on unnecessary carbohydrates. This smoothie should help any athletes in your family build lean and mean muscles as well, so you can feel confident that their nourishing diet fuels them to perform!

INGREDIENTS	INSTRUCTIONS
1 banana	Blend all the ingredients on high speed until well combined.
1 cup almond or hemp mylk	
1 cup spinach	Enjoy right away for best flavor and texture, or pour into a blender bottle for easy shakes that don't separate on the run.
1 tablespoon raw almond butter	
1 tablespoon spirulina or green protein blend	
1 tablespoon raw sweetener of choice	
1 teaspoon ground cinnamon or chopped mint leaves (both are great, providing different flavor options)	
2 tablespoons raw cacao or carob (optional)	
1 cup ice	

Makes one 16-ounce serving | RAW

ORANGE SUNRISE

Oranges are a well-loved fruit by almost all children, and seasonally, they can be a powerful immunity booster, delivering necessary vitamin C and folate. The bright citrus flavor in this smoothie is nice to complement another breakfast recipe. It's a little bit lighter in calories than some of the superfood smoothies in this chapter, yet it delivers some powerful daily nutrients.

INGREDIENTS	INSTRUCTIONS
1 banana	Blend all the ingredients on high speed until well combined.
¾ cup orange juice or fresh tangerines (whole)	Serve this smoothie immediately, or save it as an afternoon snack. It will keep well for up to 24 hours.
4 ounces almond mylk (optional)	
1 cup ice	
1 tablespoon coconut oil or hemp seeds	

Makes one 16—ounce serving

RAW

BLUEBERRY BODY & BRAIN BOOST

We have shared the powerful brain-boosting benefits of blueberries and healthy fats, but this smoothie takes these benefits and multiplies them by adding acai berry. An important source of antioxidants, the acai berry is prized for its iron and calcium content, important for all developing bodies, as well as pregnant Veggie Mamas!

INGREDIENTS	INSTRUCTIONS
1 banana	Blend all the ingredients on high speed until well combined.
1 cup blueberries	
1 cup coconut water or apple juice	Serve chilled, or leave the ice out for more of a room-temperature elixir. It's fun to serve ½-cup portions of this as a starter to a family breakfast or other meal!
⅓ cup coconut flesh (from young Thai coconut) or ¼ cup coconut shreds	
1 tablespoon acai powder	
1 tablespoon chia seeds	
1 teaspoon coconut oil	
1 teaspoon vanilla paste or powder (optional)	
1 cup ice	

Makes one 16-ounce serving

RAW

MINT MAGIC

The nice, refreshing flavor of mint qualifies this smoothie to double as a dessert or an after-meal treat. It can also be frozen as a gelato-type dessert that can be scooped out.

INGREDIENTS	INSTRUCTIONS
2 bananas	Blend all the ingredients on high speed until well combined. For a frothy smoothie, use prefrozen bananas or ice. For more of a thick mylk, leave out the ice.
1½ cups almond or pumpkin seed mylk	
½ avocado	
2 tablespoons raw coconut nectar	
1 tablespoon coconut oil (optional, will make gelato creamier)	For gelato, blend without the ice and pour the mixture into a container at least 4 inches deep that fits easily into your freezer. Freeze for 4 hours. Scoop out the gelato and enjoy!
2 tablespoons vanilla powder	
1 tablespoon chopped fresh mint leaves, 1 teaspoon dried mint leaves, or 4 drops mint extract	

Chocolate version:

⅓ cup raw cacao

1 cup ice (optional)

SUNSHINE C

This smoothie is like a ray of sunshine in a cup! Designed as a snack or to complement a meal, it's a fun blend that can be enjoyed at every stage of the developmental years and even preconception as a great foundation for the Veggie Mama lifestyle! You can creatively incorporate other superfoods of choice for additional nutritional components and to make this smoothie a balanced meal. One option we enjoy is adding 2 tablespoons ground golden flaxseeds or flax mylk.

INGREDIENTS	INSTRUCTIONS
1 cup orange juice or 6 ounces whole citrus fruits (oranges or tangerines work best for this recipe)	Blend all the ingredients on high speed until well combined. Transfer to a cup for quick and easy enjoyment, or refrigerate for later use. (Enjoy within 24 hours.)
1 cup chopped mango or papaya	
½ cup chopped pineapple	
½ cup ice	
¼ cup coconut shreds or hemp seeds	

Optional add-ins:

1 tablespoon chia seeds

1 tablespoon spirulina

1 tablespoon acai powder

Makes one 16-ounce serving | RAW

TROPICAL TWIST

Avocado is well loved as a smoothie base in Hawaii and other island communities. This smoothie is a medley of bright tropical flavors, and many young children especially enjoy the more floral tastes of tropical fruit. I (Jenny) saw this combination of pineapple and avocado on a trip to Kauai, and was surprised, but once I tried my first sip, I realized why it must be so popular—it was delicious! This smoothie also contains some extra enzymes from the pineapple and papaya that support the digestive tract, so it's beneficial during the third trimester of pregnancy as a meal or between-meal snack!

INGREDIENTS	INSTRUCTIONS
1 avocado, peeled and pitted 1 cup chopped pineapple ½ cup chopped mango or papaya 2 tablespoons hemp seeds 2 tablespoons shredded coconut 1 tablespoon sweetener of choice ½ cup water 1 cup ice	Blend all the ingredients on high speed until well combined. Enjoy right away while still chilled for the best results.

Makes one 16-ounce serving | RAW

VANILLA CRUNCH

A satisfying crunch can help break up the everyday experience of a smoothie and actually stimulates you to "chew" your sips—a necessary part of metabolic function signaling the body to begin digestion. For pregnant Veggie Mamas, smoothies are a nice option for getting in high-quality nutrition without an overly full feeling. This smoothie can be a go-to weekly option for variety!

INGREDIENTS	INSTRUCTIONS
1 banana	In a blender, combine the banana, mylk, vanilla shake powder, vanilla paste, maca root (for adults), and ice. Blend on high speed until well combined.
1 cup almond or hemp seed mylk	
⅓ cup vanilla vegan shake powder of choice (7.2 is our favorite!)	
1 tablespoon vanilla paste or powder	Add the cacao nibs and whole almonds and pulse for 10 to 15 seconds, until the nuts are broken up into small "crunch"-size pieces.
1 tablespoon maca root (mamas and papas only)	
1 cup ice	Enjoy chilled for best results.
2 tablespoons raw cacao nibs	
2 tablespoons raw almonds	

Makes one 16-ounce serving | RAW

Chapter 6

VEGGIE MAMA FRESH AND FUN FAMILY ENTRÉES

(Including Brown-Bag School Lunch Options)

Creating delicious entrées for your whole family to enjoy will require a bit of advance planning, but if you follow the steps outlined for you in Chapter 4, you will notice that this task becomes an incredible act of love that also fuels your own fire for wellness. Simply watching your kids thrive from the food you create is a great gift and makes the habit one to cherish. Consider that you are leaving a legacy of health for your children—that this is the foundation they will grow from and pass on to their own children. There is no greater gift than

that of vibrant health, especially when it includes the compassionate choice of plant-based foods that are good for your body and the planet.

Once your children learn to enjoy the fresh flavors of fruits, vegetables, nuts, and seeds in their more natural state, they break free from the addictions otherwise associated with processed foods. (As we mentioned, it's common for children to develop addictions to high-histamine foods, even if they experience an allergic reaction to them.) Our brains are wired to look for pleasure in food, and the fastest way to feel pleasure in the brain is through sugar or fat. Most processed foods are ones that quickly convert to sugar or are salty and contain saturated fats.

The brain pleasure principle is an important idea for you as a mom, especially, to understand because you should know that the challenges are not unique to you or your family! These foods are scientifically designed to trigger addiction, so when you are "weaning" your kids over to more natural foods that don't hijack their system, they will be resistant—but it's really no fault of their own.

Our children are ready for this impactful choice, and the following chapters will give you a guide to explore the tastes and textures your family will learn to love, naturally. Repetition is key. Make sure you try some of these new foods at least three times with your family. Research shows that habits are made through repetitive thought and action, and food follows this same pattern. If you are rewriting a food story with your family, we intend to bring you encouragement because we have seen from experience that keeping the door to a food opportunity open for your children is the most important aspect of transition. Since entrées, soups, salads, and snacks are more savory than sweet, you may end up spending more time fine-tuning this part of your family's diet, and you may find that sweet foods are easier to introduce. If you find that you have more resistant family members, you may wish to skip to the dessert recipes, creating new options for your family's daily enjoyment and then adding in an entrée from this chapter of the book once a week.

Many moms report that entrées and snacks can represent the most difficult part of their transitional steps. Most agree that this is an area in the past where they had relied heavily on store-bought foods that have more of the artificial tastes and processed ingredients. Therefore it's natural that this area will require the most focus, because you are working to *eliminate* artificial cravings and develop *new* tastes.

Scientifically, manufactured foods are designed to push on the pleasure pathways in the brain, creating cravings. For this reason, when you switch to more natural foods, it can be like learning to ride a bike, and you may have to develop this new love over time with "training wheels" in the form of transitional foods. Finding the right balance for your unique family and allowing everyone time to adapt to a new opportunity is the aim here. It is important to move at your own pace and respect the journey for all members of the family.

One important note: The entrées in this book are designed with balance in mind, delivering key ingredients for growing healthy families. However, if you wish to substitute out certain fruits and vegetables that are in season and local to you, that is a nice way to further bolster the health of your family and create some variety with different vitamins and minerals. Some foods that represent categories, like healthy fats (avocado, walnuts, olives, and coconut), should be substituted for other items from the same category for the best balance in the dish. If you are unsure, you can refer to our chart in the Appendix that lists different key areas of nutrition and sources.

Packing a Lunchtime Nutrient Punch

Lunches are an area of key importance for growing families. So we created this chart of lunch-box fills to show you how to use basic ingredients and combine them with some of the recipes in this book to power-pack your child's lunch! You may have a high-tech bento-style lunch box or you may be old-fashioned with your brown bag—but no matter what the container, you can be sure your child will be balanced and well fed with these food combinations! Home-made meals, besides being prepared with love and intention, are the best choice for the highest-quality nutrition. Food-service establishments and school cafeterias are not as concerned about health when it comes to their selection of ingredients or combinations of foods. For a daily routine that supports optimal wellness, it will be highly beneficial to make this switch, if you haven't already!

The following pages feature a Veggie Mama illustration of how to pack a lunch bag using very simple ingredients and the starter recipes from this book. Remember, it's all about making sure you have balanced nutrition in the bag!

PROTEINS	FRUIT AND VEGETABLE CARBOHYDRATES	ESSENTIAL FATS	OTHER: This category can help balance out the crossover between any of your categories and can be left out completely.
Raw nut and seed butters (either with apples for dipping or in a sandwich)	Cut carrots, cucumber, and/or celery	Whipped avocado or simple guacamole (for recipe, see page 154 or 152), served with Dylan's Buckwheat Crisps (page 187)	Mama's Magic Granola (page 64), dried, with Chia Coconut Fermented Yogurt (page 208)
Garbanzo or black beans	Freshly cut melons and/or berries	Olives	Sprouted-Kamut Bread (page 205)
Hummus/Tahini Cheese Spread (page 191)	Smoothies (pages 80 to 97)	Chia Coconut Fermented Yogurt (page 208)	Pumpkin Seed Cheese (page 111)
Pumpkin Protein Cakes (page 109), either alone or in a cabbage cup	Freshly cut apples, pears, peaches, pineapple, or mango	Raw nuts and seeds as a trail mix (see Nut-Free Trail Mix, page 192) or in a raw bar (see Pumpkin Seed Bars, page 190)	Quinoa
Dylan's Buckwheat Crisps (page 187)	Zucchini Noodles (page 49) with Sweet Pesto (page 53)	Chocolate Chia Pudding	Sliced baked sweet potato

MICHAEL'S MUSHROOM BURGERS

Mushrooms are a source of plant-powered protein and offer a nice texture to bite into. My (Doreen's) husband, Michael, with his love for clean food that is enjoyable and filling, provided the inspiration for this dish. These burger patties can be prepared in either an oven or a dehydrator. They are a great base item to make during your weekly prep. There are three options for wraps for the burger, and the sky's the limit for creating your own fillings to make this an "authentically yours" family dish. If you prefer sauces on your burger, add the Sweet Cheese (page 52) for a "sloppy"-style meal!

INGREDIENTS

For the mushroom patties:

4 cups whole white mushrooms

1½ cups shredded beets

1 cup cooked red quinoa

¼ cup ground dark flaxseeds

2 tablespoons minced sweet onion or 1 teaspoon onion powder

1 teaspoon minced garlic

1 teaspoon sea salt

For the wrap (choose one):

4 large romaine leaves;

4 large Napa cabbage leaves; or

4 gluten-free vegan buns

For the filling:

1 large beefsteak tomato, sliced

1 Hass avocado, peeled, pitted, and sliced

4 large butter or romaine lettuce leaves, shredded

INSTRUCTIONS

For the patties, combine all the ingredients in a food processor with the S-blade attachment in place. Process down to a thick pâté. Remove from the food processor.

Form the pâté into 5-inch round patties, ¾ inch thick.

Bake or dehydrate the patties:

For baking: Preheat the oven to 350°F while preparing the patties. Place the patties on a cookie sheet and cook until crisp on the edges, about 25 minutes.

For dehydrating: Place the patties in the dehydrator at 118°F for 6 hours until firm.

Once the patties are firm, you can begin assembly of the final meal. Layer the wrap leaves of choice or the buns with the tomato, avocado, and lettuce. Then add the patty and enjoy!

Makes 4 servings

VEGGIE TACOS WITH THREE VEGETABLE-FILLING OPTIONS

Tacos make a fun theme night or an easy buffet-style meal. Our tacos have eliminated some of the biggest challenges facing moms today by offering some simple sauces anyone can make at home and three fun vegetable combinations to change up the filling flavor and add to the creative expression of the dish. You can also try or offer different options for the taco shell. In my (Jenny's) household, half the family will use Napa cabbage leaves, while the other half will opt for sprouted-corn tortillas. Both are delicious and allow for individual tastes to be accommodated.

INGREDIENTS

For the filling options:

SUMMER TACOS

1 cup julienned cucumber

½ cup shredded carrot

½ cup shredded Napa cabbage*

½ cup quartered baby tomatoes

Sauce:
½ cup Cilantro Sauce (page 147)

SWEET TACOS

1 cup diced strawberries

1 cup diced mango or pineapple

1 cup diced avocado

¼ cup hemp seeds

Sauce:

1 cup diced strawberries

3 tablespoons water

1 tablespoon extra-virgin olive oil

1 teaspoon sea salt

SAVORY TACOS

1½ cups diced mushrooms

1 cup shredded zucchini

½ cup diced tomato

½ cup chopped spinach or kale

Sauce:

1 cup diced tomatoes

1 clove garlic

1 tablespoon chile powder

⅓ cup water

1 tablespoon extra-virgin olive oil

1 teaspoon sea salt

For the shell (choose one):

8 medium Napa cabbage or romaine lettuce leaves; or

8 sprouted-corn or brown-rice tortillas

INSTRUCTIONS

For the filling options, first prepare the sauce for one, two, or all three of these tacos. In a basic blender, blend all the ingredients on high speed until well combined. Set sauce aside until ready to use.

For all taco fillings, cut the vegetables or fruits as described and toss together in a medium bowl.

Prepare the tacos by layering the shells with the desired fillings.

Then top each taco with ¼ cup sauce.

Refrigerate leftovers for up to 4 days.

Makes 4 servings of 2 tacos each | RAW or TRANSITIONAL

QUINOA PROTEIN PASTA

This zucchini pasta noodle is fast and simple to prepare. The protein comes from the quinoa and walnuts in the dish. This is such a crowd-pleaser that we do "Pasta Wednesdays" at the Ross house regularly. Kids are creatures of habit, and this recipe offers a consistent entrée option that can be prepared in advance. This dish also can be done "buffet"-style: set up a pasta bar that you can work from, and use the optional ingredients to create variations in this dish.

INGREDIENTS	INSTRUCTIONS
For the sauce:	For the sauce, blend all the ingredients on high speed in a basic blender. Then transfer the sauce to a separate container and let sit while preparing the rest of the dish.
1 cup walnut pieces	
1 cup water	
1 Roma tomato	
⅓ cup fresh basil	For the pasta, in a large mixing bowl, combine all the pasta main ingredients. Toss together lightly.
2 tablespoons raw sweetener of choice	
2 tablespoons lemon juice	
1 teaspoon sea salt	Next, pour on the sauce and any desired optional add-ins and toss together until well combined and all the "noodles" are coated. If preparing as a buffet, leave the noodles dry and place the sauce on the side. At the end of the spread, place a bowl for tossing the ingredients together with the sauce, along with any optional add-ins.
For the pasta:	
3 zucchini, julienned, or 6 cups Zucchini Noodles (page 49)	
1½ cups cooked quinoa*	
1 cup chopped cremini mushroom	
1 cup diced Roma tomatoes or quartered baby tomatoes	To plan for this dish in advance, you can prepare the sauce and vegetables, keeping them separate until ready to serve.
Optional add-ins:	*You may elect to use sprouted, instead of cooked, quinoa for additional enzymes. If this is new for your kids, you might try doing half cooked and half sprouted quinoa to help their tastes adjust to the crunchier sprouted version. Eventually they will begin to enjoy this preparation as a nice garnish—one that packs additional protein into a variety of dishes.
½ cup sun-dried tomatoes	
½ cup artichoke hearts	
½ cup pitted kalamata olives	
½ cup diced red bell pepper	

Makes 4 servings of 2 tacos each

PUMPKIN PROTEIN CAKES

These are a family favorite for many Veggie Mamas. They are flavorful and easy to add to wraps or lettuce cups or can be enjoyed alone with a savory sauce. Here is the basic recipe that can be lightly dehydrated or just enjoyed raw after preparation.

INGREDIENTS	INSTRUCTIONS
2 cups pumpkin seeds	In a food processor with the S-blade attachment in place, combine the pumpkin seeds, quinoa, and spinach. Process these ingredients down to a coarse mixture.
1 cup sprouted** quinoa	
1 cup spinach	
½ cup diced tomatoes	Add in the tomatoes, pepper, lemon juice, and sea salt and process down further to a thick paste.
¼ cup diced red bell pepper	
¼ cup lemon juice	Using a 2-ounce ice-cream scoop, scoop out the mixture into cakes.
1 teaspoon sea salt	
⅓ cup hemp seeds	Roll the cakes in the hemp seeds.

If dehydrating, set the cakes on a dehydration tray and place in the dehydrator. Set the dehydrator at 118°F and dehydrate for 2 to 4 hours. After dehydrating, remove and enjoy fresh. Refrigerate any leftovers for up to 6 days.

*Enjoy 4 to 6 cakes as a small entrée, especially for kids, or combine with other vegetables in a lettuce cup for a larger entrée. Pumpkin seeds offer a large dose of protein per serving, so another great option is to use these cakes as a side dish or topping to boost the protein profile of entrées such as pastas, salads, and soups.

**Soak pumpkin seeds for 4 hours. Place 2 cups seeds in 2½ cups water in a glass bowl and let sit. Rinse before using.

Makes twelve 2-ounce cakes* | RAW

PUMPKIN SEED CHEESE WRAPS

Pumpkin Seed Cheese is a protein-packed spread, since pumpkin seeds are the *highest*-protein seed. These wraps make a great "fold-over" that can be eaten as a handheld option. For the wrap itself, we recommend a collard green for additional minerals, but a simple brown-rice tortilla can also be used with great results.

INGREDIENTS	INSTRUCTIONS
For the pumpkin seed cheese:	For the pumpkin seed cheese, in a blender, combine all the ingredients, loading in the liquids, spices, and vegetables, followed by the seeds, for ease of blending. Blend this mixture well until a thick, spreadable cheese is formed.
½ cup water	
¼ cup lemon juice	
1 teaspoon sea salt	
2 tablespoons chopped garlic	
1 Roma tomato	
2 cups soaked** pumpkin seeds	For the filling, in a medium mixing bowl, combine the carrot curls, zucchini, apple, and avocado. Toss together with the Tahini Sauce and set aside.
For the filling:	On a cutting board, line up all the collard greens and carefully cut out the stems.
1 cup carrot curls*	
1 cup shredded zucchini	Across the widest segment, lay one-fourth of the vegetable mix.
½ cup shredded apple	
½ cup diced Hass avocado	Top each layer of vegetable mix with one-fourth of the pumpkin seed cheese. Fold the collard green over, pressing down firmly, and serve at room temperature.
½ cup Tahini Sauce (page 141)	
4 large collard greens or brown-rice tortillas	
	If using a tortilla, fill the same way, and roll tightly around the filling.
	*Create carrot "curls" by simply using a peeler on a large carrot.
	**Soak pumpkin seeds for 4 hours. Place 2 cups seeds in 2½ cups water in a glass bowl and let sit. Rinse before using.

Makes 4 servings   RAW

HUMMUS WRAPS

This wrap uses a simple-to-prepare avocado hummus that can be a staple sauce in your weekly food rotation. For best quick-meal results with this wrap, prepare the sauce and assemble the vegetables in advance. Then when it's time to eat, you can easily pull them out and put together a 5-minute entrée.

INGREDIENTS

For the filling:

2 cups diced or thinly sliced eggplant

¼ cup extra-virgin olive oil

¼ cup chopped olives

1 tablespoon dried Italian seasoning

1 cup chopped spinach

½ cup diced tomatoes or red bell pepper

½ cup diced avocado

For the avocado hummus:

1 cup precooked garbanzo beans, well rinsed

⅓ cup lemon juice

1 clove garlic

1 teaspoon sea salt

2 tablespoons raw tahini paste

½ cup chopped avocado

4 collard green leaves, brown-rice or sprouted-corn tortillas, or paleo wraps

INSTRUCTIONS

For the filling, in a medium bowl, combine the eggplant, olive oil, olives, and dried Italian seasoning. Toss this mixture together well until the eggplant absorbs the olive oil.

Add the spinach, tomatoes, and avocado and toss together lightly. Let sit while preparing the hummus.

For the hummus, in a food processor with the S-blade attachment in place, combine the garbanzo beans, lemon juice, garlic, sea salt, and tahini paste. Process down to a thick paste.

Next, add the avocado and process down to a rich, creamy paste.

Lay out the wraps on a cutting board. If using the collard greens, remove the stems. Then spread each wrap with a layer of the hummus.

Next, evenly divide the vegetable mixture on top of the hummus.

Finally, roll each wrap tightly around the vegetables and enjoy fresh.

Makes 4 servings, plus an additional 8 ounces hummus for later use | RAW

VEGGI-WICHES

The best part about these sandwiches is creating an interesting look with your veggie cuts. Preparing sandwiches the Veggie Mama way means ensuring a well-balanced meal by including proteins, essential fatty acids, and a variety of vitamins and minerals from different fruits and vegetables. This recipe fills the bill to a T!

INGREDIENTS	INSTRUCTIONS
For the filling: 1 mango 1 avocado 1 cucumber 1 cup carrot curls 1 beefsteak tomato 1 cup Tahini Cheese Spread (page 191) **For the wrap** **(choose one):** 8 slices sprouted brown-rice bread; 8 slices Sprouted-Kamut Bread (page 205); or 8 large romaine or butter lettuce leaves	For the filling, cut the mango, avocado, and cucumber into long, thin pieces. It's easy to create carrot curls by simply peeling a large carrot. For the cucumber, tomato, and avocado, try cutting across the fruits and vegetables lengthwise, yielding large, flat pieces ¼ inch thick. Once the vegetables are prepared, lay out 4 slices sprouted-grain bread or lettuce leaves and layer ¼ cup Tahini Cheese Spread on each. Top with layers of each fruit and vegetable. Place the remaining 4 bread slices or lettuce leaves on top and press down so the sandwich is firmly together. You may elect to spear with a fun sandwich pick for a little flair!

Makes 4 servings

VEGGIE MAMA STACKS

Stacks are a great way to get in lots of fruits and vegetables without attracting too much notice. With a stacked dish like this one, the simple towers of food can be enjoyed as a main or side dish, but they take away the monotony of the vegetables by creating a unique look.

INGREDIENTS	INSTRUCTIONS
For the sauce:	For the sauce, in a basic blender, combine the tahini spread and tomato and blend until well combined.
1 cup Tahini Cheese Spread (page 191)	
1 Roma tomato, chopped	
	For the stacks, in a medium mixing bowl, toss all the stack ingredients with the sauce until well combined.
For the stacks:	
4 cups julienned cucumber	Then, using a ring mold, compress 2 cups of the mixture and press down firmly until compact. (Ring molds can be found at kitchen-supply stores and look like mini cheesecake pans; if you don't have one, you can use a small shallow bowl to layer the vegetables.) Invert the mold onto a plate and press out the stack. Repeat to make 4 stacks.
1 cup shredded beets	
1 cup diced avocado	
1 cup finely chopped kale	
1 cup white corn kernels (optional)	
¼ cup hemp seeds (optional for garnish)	
2 tablespoons dulse flakes (optional for garnish)	Garnish with additional functional foods, like hemp seeds or dulse flakes.

Makes 4 servings | RAW

FAMILY FLATBREAD

This recipe is a "no bake" flatbread made using a simple crust of buckwheat flour. The toppings are our favorite combination, but you can also create your own version based on the preferences of your family.

INGREDIENTS	INSTRUCTIONS

For the crust:

1 Roma tomato

1 red bell pepper

1 teaspoon sea salt

1 cup water

2 tablespoons extra-virgin olive oil

2 cups buckwheat flour

⅓ cup ground golden flaxseeds

For the topping:

2 cups diced mixed mushrooms

1 cup diced pitted kalamata olives

1 cup Marinara (page 159)

¼ cup Rawmesan Cheese (page 160)

1 cup carrot curls

For the crust, in a blender, combine the tomato, bell pepper, sea salt, water, and olive oil. Blend down to a thin consistency.

Then place the buckwheat flour and flaxseeds in a food processor with the S-blade attachment in place. Turn on the processor and begin adding in the mixture from the blender, processing until a dough ball forms.

Remove the dough ball and press out to a 7 × 7-inch square, ½ inch thick.

For the topping, in a medium mixing bowl, combine the mushrooms, olives, Marinara, and Rawmesan Cheese, and toss well until the mushrooms absorb the sauce. Evenly spread this mixture out over the flatbread. Top with the carrot curls.

If you would like to warm the flatbread, place on a pizza stone in an oven preheated to 250°F. Bake for 10 minutes with the door cracked for best results.

Makes 4 servings

SWEET YAMS AND RICE

Yams are a nice departure from potatoes and offer an increased selection of important minerals benefiting bone development! Yams are also known to increase fertility so this is a fun dish to incorporate throughout your parenting process. The rice mixture in this dish can also be easily saved to incorporate into other dishes throughout the week so you may wish to double or triple the rice batch so you can cook once and enjoy all week long!

INGREDIENTS	INSTRUCTIONS
For the yams:	Preheat the oven to 350°F.
4 cups sliced yams	Prepare the yam segment of the dish by blending the agave, oil, sea salt, and cinnamon.
½ cup raw agave nectar	
¼ cup olive oil	
1 teaspoon sea salt	Toss the yams in this mixture, coating each segment, and lay them flat on a nonstick baking sheet or in a shallow glass baking dish.
1 teaspoon ground cinnamon (optional)	
For the rice:	Bake for 45 minutes until the yams are cooked all the way through. Pierce with a fork to ensure the yams are soft before removing. *Note:* Check doneness at 35 to 40 minutes, as moister yams will cook more rapidly than drier yams.
4 cups cooked basmati rice*	
2 cups chopped raw kale	
½ cup finely chopped walnuts	
½ cup diced red bell pepper	
½ cup shredded carrots	Prepare the sauce for the rice by blending all ingredients until well combined.
	In a mixing bowl, toss together the warm rice and sauce until well combined.
For the rice sauce:	
1 cup diced red bell peppers	Add in the kale, walnuts, and bell pepper and toss again.
2 tablespoons coconut aminos	
2 tablespoons raw agave nectar	Remove the yams from the oven.
2 tablespoons extra-virgin olive oil	To serve, scoop the rice mixture on top of the yams, layered in a bowl, or place
1 teaspoon sea salt	

INSTRUCTIONS, CONT'D.

the entire mixture onto a platter with the yams around the rice for group serving. Enjoy warm.

Refrigerate leftovers for up to 5 days.

*While the yams are baking, cook the basmati rice: Bring 4 cups of water to a boil on the stove top. Add 2 cups rice to the pot, lower heat to a simmer, then cover and cook for 15 minutes.

Makes 8 cups

Veggie Mama Idea for the Adventurous Family:
The Family That Gardens Together . . .

There's no better-tasting food than organic vegetables and fruits that you grow in your own backyard. Involving your children with building, maintaining, and harvesting your garden will definitely instill enthusiasm for the homegrown foods.

It's easy to grow a lush and productive organic garden in small spaces, too! You can simply buy hydroponic kits for use inside your home, and grow tomatoes, peas, strawberries, and other delights in planter boxes on your balcony or patio. In addition, look for "vertical gardens," akin to flowerpots that hang on a burlap cloth, enabling you to grow produce on any wall.

When you grow a garden, it's helpful to consider which plants will be enjoyable eaten together so that you'll be able to make at least one whole dish entirely from your garden!

ROW CROPS	TRELLIS CROPS	HERBS
Baby Leaf lettuces	Green snap peas	Cilantro
Curly kale	Baby eggplant	Parsley
Squash	Blackberries	Garlic

Chapter 7

VEGGIE MAMA MIX-AND-MATCH SOUPS, SALADS, SAUCES, AND SIDES

What makes small bites, soups, and salads different from an entrée? Not much! These particular dishes are designed to be enjoyed together to collectively create a meal, individually in large portions as an entrée, or as easy "add-ons" to shared meals. Also, the sauces in this chapter can fuel a variety of unique dishes that are custom creations throughout your week, potentially using leftovers in a new way. A favorite wintertime meal of ours is the Tomato Basil Bisque with the Sweet Kale Salad. The Veggie Chowder and Lentil Soup are filling, with additional toppings to round out a meal, and also pair nicely with the pasta dishes in the book. The Cilantro Sauce is absolutely "to live for" and makes a great sauce to fold into steamed quinoa. You can mix and match these dishes a bit easier than the full entrées, so try your hand at experimenting!

Soups and Salads

One crafty Veggie Mama idea is to pre-prepare your salads, like the Cucumber and Dill Salad, and place them in individual serving sizes in mason jars. Even salads with leafy greens can be layered in a jar like in this image and make for a fast and easy meal on the run.

Soups too can be a great pre-prep item that can be individually portioned so that anyone, even older siblings charged with the care of a younger brother or sister, can grab and reheat easily.

LENTIL SOUP

·◈·

Lentils are more easily digested than other types of legumes, offering a healthy source of dietary fiber. This soup is a perfect slow cooker meal and can also be made on the stove top. You can then garnish with fresh, living vegetables like shredded carrots or beets for color and additional active enzymes.

INGREDIENTS	INSTRUCTIONS
1½ cups dried lentils	If preparing on the stove top, combine all the ingredients in a large stockpot. Bring the mixture to a boil and then lower the heat and let simmer, covered, for approximately 45 minutes.
6 cups vegetable stock	
1 cup diced yellow crookneck squash	
1 Roma tomato or red bell pepper, diced	
1 brown onion, diced	Stir the soup every 15 minutes or so to prevent the lentils from caking. Let sit, covered, on low heat for the last 15 minutes without stirring.
1 cup diced celery	
2 cups diced carrots	
2 cloves garlic, minced	If using a slow cooker, place all the ingredients in the pot and heat on medium for 4 to 6 hours, depending on your equipment. Check after 4 hours and monitor in ½-hour increments for the final 2 hours.
1 tablespoon sea salt	
Pepper to taste	
⅓ cup shredded fresh root vegetables, for garnish	
	Garnish the dish with the fresh shredded root vegetables for more color, flavor, and nutrition.
	Leftovers? Blend this soup in a basic blender until well combined for a delicious lentil gravy you can serve over vegetables.

Makes 4 servings

TOMATO BASIL BISQUE

This is a nice rich, creamy soup but with no cream! The trick here is to add the oil while blending as the last step in order to quickly emulsify the soup. Try this with your kids and have them watch how the color changes.

INGREDIENTS

4 cups warm water

3 cups chopped Roma tomato

⅓ cup fresh basil

2 cloves garlic

2 tablespoons dried Italian seasoning

2 tablespoons raw agave nectar or coconut nectar

1 teaspoon sea salt

¼ cup extra-virgin olive oil

INSTRUCTIONS

In the blender, combine the water, tomato, basil, garlic, seasoning, agave nectar, and salt, and blend on high speed until well combined.

Once you have a creamy blend, add the final ingredient, the olive oil, while blending and watch as the color changes and the soup thickens up.

Serve this warm from the blender, or place in the dehydrator set on high until ready to serve. Refrigerate the leftovers and heat in the dehydrator or on the stove top on low until warm to the touch. This soup will keep for up to 4 days in the refrigerator.

Makes 6 cups

RAW

VEGGIE CHOWDER

This chowder is so fast to whip up! It's a raw soup that can be warmed according to your preferred taste and, for your Veggie Mama convenience, can be made well in advance!

INGREDIENTS

4 cups sweet white corn (optional)

2 cups chopped yellow squash

1 cup carrot juice

1 cup almond or sunflower mylk (optional, makes thicker)

2 tablespoons extra-virgin olive oil

2 tablespoons miso paste

2 tablespoons nutritional yeast

1 teaspoon garlic powder

1 teaspoon onion powder

1 teaspoon sea salt

INSTRUCTIONS

In a blender, combine 2 cups of the white corn, squash, carrot juice, almond mylk, olive oil, miso paste, nutritional yeast, garlic and onion powders, and sea salt. Blend on high speed until well combined.

Add in the remaining 2 cups white corn and lightly blend, leaving some small chunky pieces.

Serve lightly warmed or even chilled.

Refrigerate and use this soup all week long for an easy grab-and-go meal.

Makes six 8-ounce servings

ENERGY SPLIT-PEA SOUP

Split peas are high in protein, and this soup is also high in important minerals. This soup makes a nice side or starter dish, and it can stand alone as a meal with the addition of garnishes like sea vegetables or a sprinkling of nuts and seeds. This is a nice transitional recipe that adds a raw oil at the end of preparation. That two-step technique will save having to heat the oil past the optimal point for consumption! This is a Veggie Mama trick everyone should know because it will support your family's cardiovascular health, which can be harmed by cooked oils. You can use this technique with other recipes easily for optimal hearth-healthy meals!

INGREDIENTS	INSTRUCTIONS
8 cups water	Combine the water, asparagus, split peas, onion, and garlic in a medium stockpot on the stove. Heat the mixture over medium heat and slowly bring to a boil.
4 cups diced asparagus	
2 cups split peas	
1 cup diced brown onion	
2 cloves garlic	Let boil for 5 to 7 minutes, then lower to a simmer and cook until the split peas are soft.
¼ cup extra-virgin olive oil	
	Transfer the mixture to a blender and blend on high speed until rich and creamy. Then, while blending, add the olive oil to help emulsify the mixture.
	Serve the soup warm. Save all leftovers for up to 7 days in the refrigerator.

Makes 6 servings

MARVELOUS MISO SOUP

Miso is a great ingredient to boost your family's immune system, so we included a very basic version of this soup in your weekly meal-planning section. However, once you get going making these fresh foods routinely, you will want to try swapping it out for this version, which includes more complex flavors. This is a recipe we use all the time because it is quick and easy to reproduce and makes use of extra leftover pieces of zucchini and Napa cabbage!

INGREDIENTS	INSTRUCTIONS
For the broth:	For the broth, in a blender, combine the broth ingredients and blend on high speed until warm (you may wish to use already warm water for a hotter soup).
6 cups water	
2 tablespoons mellow white miso paste	
2 tablespoons Tahini Cheese Spread (page 191)	Divide the noodles, coconut, cabbage, and carrots evenly among 6 cups and pour the broth over the top.
1 teaspoon sea salt	
For the filling:	Sprinkle the green onion and sesame seeds over the top of each serving before sharing with friends and family.
4 cups Zucchini Noodles (page 49)	
1 cup thin strips coconut meat (optional)	
1 cup shredded cabbage	
½ cup shredded carrots	
4 tablespoons chopped green onion	
1 tablespoon sesame seeds	

Makes 6 servings | RAW

VEGETABLE MINESTRONE SOUP

Vegetable soup is a nice option for the winter season. This recipe is oil-free, so it is more supportive of overall heart health yet is still rich and hearty, relying on the combined natural flavors of the fresh vegetables. In-the-know Veggie Mamas see this as a family-favorite option for weekly food preparation, and a great place to add in the vegetable scraps used in other preparations throughout the week. For this reason, this soup has been dubbed "Sunday soup" and is always open for more vegetable additions!

INGREDIENTS	INSTRUCTIONS
4 cups water	In a blender, blend the water, tomato, and squash until well combined.
1 cup chopped Roma tomato	
1 cup diced squash	Transfer the liquid to a large stockpot or slow cooker.
1 cup diced celery	
1 cup diced carrot	Add the remaining vegetables, garbanzo beans, and seasonings to the mixture.
1 cup diced sweet potatoes	
¼ cup chopped onion	Heat on low on the stove top for 1 hour or in a slow cooker for 4 hours.
2 tablespoons chopped garlic	
1 cup garbanzo beans	Enjoy this soup warm. Take it along in a lunch-box thermos or refrigerate until the next at-home use.
2 tablespoons dried Italian seasoning	
2 bay leaves	
1 tablespoon sea salt	

Makes 6 servings

COCONUT CRÈME SOUP

This soup is enjoyable warm or chilled and also makes a great sauce for Asian and Zucchini Noodle dishes. We recommend making a double batch, as this is another great base recipe, storable in the refrigerator for up to 7 days. Since we are preparing a broth to pour over fresh ingredients, you can make this a fun variable experience by changing the ingredients or allowing your family to add in their own favorites to make a unique dish!

INGREDIENTS	INSTRUCTIONS
For the broth:	For the broth, in a basic blender, blend the ingredients on high speed until well combined.
2½ cups coconut water or hot water	
1 cup thinly sliced coconut meat	
⅓ cup lime juice	For the soup bowls, layer the fresh ingredients among 4 bowls and then pour in the soup broth. Enjoy warm or chilled.
1 tablespoon mellow white miso paste	
1 pinch sea salt	
For the fresh soup bowl:	
1 cup shredded carrots	
2 cups kelp noodles or Zucchini Noodles (page 49)	
1 cup chopped spinach or cabbage	
1 cup enoki mushrooms	
1 cup diced avocado	
Chopped green onions, for garnish	

Makes 4 cups

FRUIT SALAD

Cinnamon and spinach? Yes, it's true—these are both highly alkalizing foods rarely found together, but this fruit salad defies the odds and combines the best of the spice and vegetable worlds!

INGREDIENTS

For the dressing:

2 tablespoons extra-virgin olive oil

2 tablespoons apple juice

2 teaspoons ground cinnamon

1 pinch sea salt

For the salad:

2 cups chopped spinach

1 cup thinly sliced Gala or green apple

1 cup diced banana

1 cup diced strawberries, sliced grapes, or sliced mango

1 cup diced avocado

2 tablespoons coconut flakes

2 tablespoons hemp seeds

INSTRUCTIONS

For the dressing, in a medium mixing bowl, combine all the ingredients and whisk together with a fork.

For the salad, add all the salad ingredients to the bowl with the dressing. Toss the mixture together well and serve in chilled bowls for the best results.

In the summer, you might want to use frozen grapes to add a fun textural element to the salad.

Refrigerate leftovers and be sure to use within 3 days.

Makes 6 servings

RAW

SWEET KALE SALAD

If you can create a marinated kale that has a sweet flavor to it, there is a better opportunity for introducing this essential green to even the pickiest of eaters. There are two keys for success: (1) Use healthy oils to coat finely chopped kale in order to create a nice soft leaf that is easy to chew; and (2) create a dressing that livens up the naturally bitter notes of the kale in order to offset it and create a unique flavor that is special to this salad in particular.

INGREDIENTS

For the dressing:

½ cup extra-virgin olive oil

¼ cup lemon juice

¼ cup apple juice

2 drops stevia or 1 tablespoon raw coconut nectar or raw honey

1 pinch sea salt

For the salad:

4 cups finely chopped kale

½ diced Hass avocado

½ cup red grapes or raisins

½ cup thinly sliced Gala apple

¼ cup walnut pieces

INSTRUCTIONS

For the dressing, combine all the ingredients in a basic blender and blend on high speed until well combined. Alternatively, you may whisk this together well.

For the salad, in a medium mixing bowl, combine the kale, avocado, and dressing and massage the mixture together using tongs.

Then cut the grapes in half lengthwise and cut the apples down into matchstick shapes.

Add the remaining ingredients to the bowl and toss well.

This salad is hearty and holds together well. You may elect to use a ring mold to compress the salad and create salad "stacks" at the time of serving for an interesting presentation that delights the whole family!

Makes 4 side-salad or 2 entrée servings | RAW

LAGUNA SALAD

The two of us Veggie Mamas originally met in the city of Laguna Beach, California. We both found the art and diversity of the culture there lent itself to unique combinations of food, as well as a laid-back, easygoing beachy lifestyle! This recipe was inspired by the coastline where this recipe emerged. The fresh flavors combined with the life-giving energy of the salad itself make this snack a great refresher after an afternoon in the ocean!

INGREDIENTS	INSTRUCTIONS
For the dressing:	For the dressing, in a medium mixing bowl, combine all the ingredients and whisk together.
2 tablespoons stone-ground mustard	
2 tablespoons apple cider vinegar	For the salad, add the jicama, tangerine, and butter lettuce to the bowl with the dressing and toss until well coated. Layer the salad onto a plate.
2 tablespoons raw coconut nectar	
1 pinch sea salt	
2 tablespoons fresh orange juice (optional)	Top with the diced avocado and hemp seeds.
For the salad:	
2 cups shredded jicama	
½ cup tangerine segments	
2 cups chopped butter lettuce	
1 cup diced avocado	
2 tablespoons hemp seeds	

Makes 4 servings

RAW

TANGERINE SALAD

Tangerines are an enticing way to create a salad that is bright and attracts young children to salad. You can use a few helpful tricks by adding nutrient-dense sprouts and super foods to the salad to increase it's nutritional benefits as well without compromising taste. Hemp seeds and sunflower sprouts both work well in this salad and can serve as a great introduction for these ingredients in other recipes as well. This salad is also nice as a filling in wraps and over fresh spinach for an alternative presentation.

INGREDIENTS

For the dressing:

¼ cup orange juice

¼ cup olive oil or avocado oil

1 teaspoon raw coconut nectar

1 teaspoon miso paste

1 teaspoon finely chopped green onions (leave out for kids sensitive to spices)

½ teaspoon sea salt

For the salad:

3 cups peeled and segmented tangerines

3 cups cubed cucumbers

⅓ cup hemp seeds

1 cup sunflower, clover, or broccoli sprouts (optional)

INSTRUCTIONS

Whisk all dressing ingredients together well in a medium bowl.

Add in the tangerines, cucumbers, and sprouts and toss together well.

Serve the salad fresh or chilled. Garnish with hemp seeds and sprouts just prior to serving.

Makes 6 cups

RAW

CUCUMBER AND DILL SALAD

This is a great hydrating and cooling salad that can easily double as a topping over a green salad or as a filling for a wrap.

INGREDIENTS

For the dressing:

½ Hass avocado

¼ cup lemon juice

2 tablespoons nutritional yeast

1 cup water

1 teaspoon sea salt

For the salad:

8 Persian cucumbers, diced

2 cups baby tomatoes, cut into quarters

2 tablespoons fresh dill

INSTRUCTIONS

For the dressing, in a basic blender, combine the dressing ingredients and blend on high speed until well combined. Then transfer to a medium mixing bowl.

For the salad, add the cucumber, tomatoes, and dill to the bowl with the dressing and toss together well.

Chill this salad before serving for best results.

Sauces and Sides

Sides make for simple dishes to pre-portion and pack to take on playdates and more! Tip to the wise Veggie Mama: If you are unsure at first about how much to make for your growing family, choose the heartier dishes like the Broccoli Pesto Quinoa, and after you see what the rate of consumption is on that particular dish, you can always freeze the rest and have it to come back to the following week. While this won't work for salads, it's a great way to get more mileage out of your soups, grain and legume dishes, and dressings.

Many moms ask if there is any nutritional benefit lost in the process of freezing. The USDA Table of Nutrient Retention Factors (2003) suggests that really only 5 percent of the nutrient components are lost in most vitamins (except vitamin C, which ranks at 30 percent), and nearly all of the nutrient factors are still present in the minerals. Each vitamin and mineral is affected differently, but overall, freezing is a much more nutrient-rich way of preserving food compared with cooking, and even drying!

CILANTRO DRESSING

This dressing tends to be naturally on the sweeter side and is a basic flavor that easily combines with all types of dishes. You can store this dressing for up to 7 days in the refrigerator, so it is easy to prepare in advance and use throughout the week for extra flavor in your favorite dishes.

INGREDIENTS	INSTRUCTIONS
1⅓ cups extra-virgin olive oil	Blend all the ingredients in a high-powered blender.
⅔ cup cilantro leaves	
⅔ cup lemon juice	Transfer the dressing to a mason jar or container for storage in the refrigerator.
2 cloves garlic	
1 teaspoon sea salt	

Makes 2 cups

RAW

TAHINI SAUCE

Tahini is an iron-rich base for thick sauces, and this recipe is an all-around flavor that is easy to interchange in dishes. You might try it with the Pumpkin Seed Bars (page 190) for a simple snack. This sauce will store for 5 days in the refrigerator.

INGREDIENTS	INSTRUCTIONS
½ cup raw tahini paste	In a basic blender, blend all the ingredients until well combined.
¼ cup diced Roma tomato	
¼ cup lemon juice	Transfer the sauce to a mason jar or easy container for storage in the refrigerator.
¼ cup water	
2 tablespoons chopped green onion	
2 basil leaves	
1 clove garlic	
1 teaspoon sea salt	
Additional spices as desired, such as dill, light chile powder, or cilantro for flavor variation	

Makes 1 1/2 cups | RAW

SWEET GINGER SAUCE

Ginger is an anti-inflammatory ingredient with a strong flavor. When you prepare this recipe, you can add in more ginger juice 1 teaspoon at a time until the desired taste is achieved. This sauce is great for dipping or adding an Asian flair to vegetable sides.

INGREDIENTS	INSTRUCTIONS
½ cup coconut aminos	Whisk all the ingredients in a medium mixing bowl or blend on low in a basic blender until well combined. Store for up to 7 days in the refrigerator.
⅓ cup lime juice	
2 tablespoons ginger juice	
2 tablespoons raw agave nectar or coconut nectar	

Makes 1 cup

ALFREDO SAUCE

Alfredo will add a nice flavor and texture to a vegetable side, or it can be a base ingredient on a pasta bar! This recipe includes options for creative uses. The sauce must be refrigerated and can keep for a maximum of 5 days, so it is best prepared weekly or fresh.

INGREDIENTS	INSTRUCTIONS
1 cup soaked cashews or pine nuts 1 cup coconut water 1 clove garlic ¼ cup nutritional yeast 1 teaspoon sea salt	Blend all the ingredients in a high-powered blender for a rich, creamy sauce. Refrigerate until ready to use. *Filling option:* Whisk in 2 tablespoons psyllium husk to thicken the sauce. Use this for filling vegetables like Deviled Tomatoes (page 153). *Red option:* Add ½ cup sun-dried tomatoes to the blender for a rich red sauce.

Makes 2 cups

BROCCOLI PESTO QUINOA

·❖·

For the Veggie Mama or family member who enjoys a savory treat, this is a fun and flavorful way to get in the alkalizing effects of broccoli and the plant-power protein of quinoa. This blend can easily be made in advance by dehydrating or lightly cooking and then be stored in the refrigerator for up to 4 days for an easy grab-and-go meal.

INGREDIENTS

For the pesto:

½ cup extra-virgin olive oil

⅔ cup fresh basil leaves

4 cloves garlic

1 teaspoon sea salt

1 cup walnuts or pistachios

For the entrée:

4 cups broccoli florets

6 cups cooked or sprouted quinoa

½ cup diced Roma tomato or red bell pepper

INSTRUCTIONS

For the pesto, in a blender, combine the olive oil, basil, garlic, and sea salt. Blend well until a green emulsion is formed.

Add in the nuts and blend well until a thick pesto sauce is formed. Remove the sauce from the blender and set aside.

For the entrée, in a steamer basket on the stove top, lightly steam the broccoli for 7 minutes.*

Then, in a medium mixing bowl, combine the quinoa, broccoli, and Roma

INSTRUCTIONS, CONT'D.

tomato. Toss the mixture together until well combined.

Now pour the pesto sauce over the vegetable mixture and toss until well coated.

Serve up this fresh mix alongside another favorite vegetable dish or as an entrée. If enjoying as an entrée, we recommend garnishing it with more essential fats from either olives or avocado or even adding Zucchini Noodles (page 49) or chopped spinach. You can add more protein by sprinkling with hemp seeds.

*Alternatively, for a raw meal, you can prepare the broccoli in the dehydrator following these steps:

After blending the pesto, combine the pesto and broccoli florets in a medium mixing bowl and toss together well.

Spread this mixture on a covered tray and place in the dehydrator for 4 hours at 118°F. Remove the mixture from the dehydrator and place in a medium mixing bowl.

Add the quinoa and tomato and toss together. Serve straight from the dehydrator for a warm yet still raw snack!

Makes 4 servings

RAW or TRANSITIONAL

EASY WRAPS

Use these easy wraps to have around for side dishes and to fill with leftovers for a quick meal. They are called for in a few of the recipes in this book, but they are a kitchen staple. These are made in the dehydrator, and once you get used to preparing them, you will find that they are easy and simple to create. We use the Sedona dehydrator for best results with this recipe, but you can use any dehydrator that has a raw setting of less than 125°F. Because a dehydrator functions differently than an oven, even when it is set at 125°F, the food inside is barely being heated at 118°F, so this is considered a raw-foods setting.

INGREDIENTS	INSTRUCTIONS
1 cup water 3 cups cubed zucchini 1 cup shredded carrots 1 cup ground golden flaxseeds 2 tablespoons Italian seasoning (optional)	In a basic blender, combine all the ingredients, adding in the water and vegetables first, followed by the flaxseeds and Italian seasoning, if using. Blend on high speed until well combined. Line a dehydrator tray with a nonstick drying sheet. Spread the mixture out evenly to cover the surface of the dehydration tray. Place in the dehydrator set at 118°F until dry to the touch. When dry, remove the wraps and flip them over. Place back in the dehydrator and dry for up to 1 hour. Remove from the dehydrator. If your wraps are unevenly dry, or appear crispier in one area over another, you can take a damp paper towel or cheesecloth and lay it gently over the wrap for 15 minutes. It should soften up and again become pliable for use. Store these in the refrigerator for best results. This will keep them soft and moist. Use within a 6-week window.

Makes 1 tray, approximately 4 wraps

RAW

SWEET ROOT-VEGETABLE QUINOA

✥

This is another fun and inviting way to enjoy quinoa that is colorful and with a mild yet savory finish. This dish boasts more than 18 grams of protein per serving!

INGREDIENTS

For the cilantro sauce:

½ cup extra-virgin olive oil

⅓ cup cilantro leaves

1 clove garlic

¼ cup lemon juice

1 tablespoon raw coconut or agave nectar

1 teaspoon sea salt

For the vegetable mix:

6 cups cooked tricolor quinoa

½ cup shredded carrots

½ cup shredded red beets

½ cup diced tomato

4 tablespoons chopped green onion

1 tablespoon cilantro leaves

1 teaspoon sea salt

INSTRUCTIONS

For the sauce, in a blender, combine all the sauce ingredients and blend on high speed until well mixed. Remove the sauce and set aside until ready to use.

For the vegetable mix, in a large saucepan, combine the quinoa, vegetables, green onion, and cilantro leaves with 1 cup of the cilantro sauce and sea salt.

Heat on low for 3 to 5 minutes, until the mixture is lightly warmed. Remove from the heat and serve right away.

You can enjoy this mixture all week long by combining the sauce and veggie mix and then just lightly warming to order.

Makes 4 servings, plus an extra 1/4 cup sauce

SWEET STUFFED MUSHROOMS

This is a savory blend with a hint of sweetness to please developing taste buds. These mushrooms are a great option prepared before a busy weekend because they travel well and can be created in advance of events and then stored until the time of entertaining.

INGREDIENTS

12 cleaned cremini mushroom caps

3 tablespoons extra-virgin olive oil

For the filling:

2 cups walnut pieces

1 teaspoon sea salt

2 tablespoons coconut aminos

2 tablespoons raw sweetener of choice

⅓ cup chopped fresh basil

½ cup diced Roma tomato

½ cup diced red bell pepper

3 tablespoons extra-virgin olive oil

INSTRUCTIONS

In a medium mixing bowl, combine the cremini mushrooms and olive oil and toss to coat. Gently skim the surface of each mushroom, ensuring that all main sides are coated with olive oil.

Transfer the mushrooms to a dehydration tray and set with the open side facing up.*

INSTRUCTIONS, CONT'D.

For the filling, in a food processor with the S-blade attachment in place, grind the walnuts into a meal. Remove the meal and place in a mixing bowl.

Add the sea salt, coconut aminos, sweetener, and chopped basil and fold together.

In the food processor with the S-blade attachment still in place, process the tomato, red bell pepper, and olive oil into a chunky, chutney-style mixture. Add in the walnut mixture and pulse to a stuffing-like consistency.

Fill the mushrooms evenly with the mixture and then place the tray in the dehydrator.

Dehydrate at 118°F for 4 to 6 hours, until nice and soft. The flavors should combine, softening the mushroom caps completely.

*Alternatively, you can follow the same steps in this recipe but bake the mushrooms instead at 250°F for 25 minutes for a similar result. While it's preferable to enjoy these out of the dehydrator for the highest concentration of nutrients, it's still an enjoyable transitional dish out of the oven.

Makes 12 mushrooms

RAW or TRANSITIONAL

SOUTH OF THE BORDER BAKED CRISPS, SWEET SALSA, AND GREEN GUACAMOLE

This snack features sauces that can be integrated into other meals or used as condiments throughout the week. If your family is gluten-free, this is a great dish for you, especially if you get some healthy tortillas to work with!

INGREDIENTS

For the baked crisps:

1 package of 8 organic brown-rice tortillas*

1 tablespoon chile garlic salt or sea salt

1 lime wedge

For the salsa:

6 tomatillos, husked, washed, and diced

2 green onions, roots removed

⅓ cup fresh cilantro

½ cup lemon juice

1 teaspoon raw honey

1 teaspoon sea salt

1 serrano pepper (optional)

For the guacamole:

2 Hass avocados, peeled and pitted

1 lemon or lime

Pepper to taste

1 teaspoon dulse flakes

¼ cup chopped cilantro, for garnish (optional)

INSTRUCTIONS

For the crisps, preheat the oven to 350°F.

Cut the tortillas into quarters. In a medium mixing bowl, toss the tortillas, creating space between each. Then sprinkle with the chile garlic salt and squeeze the lime wedge over the bowl. Using your fingers, disperse the salt and the lime juice loosely over the tortilla pieces.

Line up the tortilla pieces on a cookie sheet so they do not overlap. Place in the oven for 7 minutes. Remove the cookie sheet and, using tongs, flip over each tortilla; place back in the oven for 7 to 10 minutes, until crispy.

Remove the tortillas and let cool. These crisps will store easily in your pantry in an airtight container for up to 2 weeks.

For the salsa, add all the ingredients to a basic food processor with the S-blade attachment in place, and pulse to the desired consistency. (Your family may enjoy a chunky salsa or more of a salsa puree.)

INSTRUCTIONS, CONT'D

Remove the salsa from the food processor and refrigerate until ready to use. This salsa will keep for up to 3 days in the refrigerator.

For the guacamole, first place the sea salt and the avocado in a small bowl. Using the back of a fork, smash the avocado over and over until a chunky spread has formed. Now squeeze the lemon over the avocado and fold into the mixture along with the dulse flakes. If you enjoy a little heat in your guacamole, fold in the pepper, tasting as you go until the desired flavor is achieved. Garnish the guacamole with the fresh cilantro, if desired.

Serve the guacamole and the salsa surrounded by the baked tortillas. This makes an easy and light spring meal alongside an entrée soup or salad and can be a great pot-luck dish to share with friends.

Nutrition note: Brown-rice tortillas are the preferred choice according to Veggie Mama philosophy. However, if these are unavailable and you need to go with corn tortillas, you should know how to shop for them, as corn tortillas come in many varieties. It is important to read the labels. You want a tortilla made from simple organic corn, lime, and salt. There is really no need for other ingredients. Do your best to look for as few ingredients as possible in your corn tortillas, and if you can find them sprouted, they will be easier to digest.

Makes 4 appetizer servings

TUESDAY TOSTADAS

We love Tuesday Tostadas in our Veggie Mama household because they are a simple combination of pre-prepped components that can keep your healthy routine moving strong to start the week out right.

INGREDIENTS

For the simple guacamole:

1 Hass avocado, peeled and pitted

¼ cup lemon juice

1 teaspoon sea salt

For the tostadas:

4 tostada shells (choose between baked brown-rice tortillas or Dylan's Buckwheat Crisps [page 187])

4 cups shredded romaine lettuce

4 cups Veggie Mix (page 49)

1 cup Tahini Sauce (page 141)

INSTRUCTIONS

For the guacamole, in a small mixing bowl, smash the avocado flesh using a fork. Then add the lemon juice and sea salt and continue to smash the avocado mixture into a smooth guacamole.

For the tostadas, if baking the tostada shells, follow the instructions on page 150 of the South of the Border Baked Crisps and let cool. Line up all the tostada shells on a cutting board.

Evenly divide the guacamole among the shells.

Top the guacamole with the shredded romaine lettuce, followed by the Veggie Mix, and finally the Tahini Sauce.

Serve the tostadas fresh and enjoy with addition sprinkles of sea salt or cayenne pepper for a little spice.

Makes 4 servings (can be adjusted by adding more of each item for additional family members)

DEVILED TOMATOES

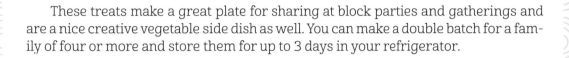

These treats make a great plate for sharing at block parties and gatherings and are a nice creative vegetable side dish as well. You can make a double batch for a family of four or more and store them for up to 3 days in your refrigerator.

INGREDIENTS	INSTRUCTIONS
6 medium Roma tomatoes 1 cup diced red bell pepper (optional) 2 cups Alfredo Sauce (page 143) 1 teaspoon ground cumin, for garnish	On a cutting board, cut the Roma tomatoes in half lengthwise. Then, using a tablespoon, remove the seeds and cores and set aside for use in a soup or sauce recipe. If using red bell peppers, whisk them into the Alfredo Sauce prior to filling. Lay the tomatoes out on the cutting board and fill evenly with the sauce. Top with a sprinkle of cumin and serve chilled. *Crisp option:* If you have a dehydrator, dehydrate the tomatoes at 118°F for 2 hours. Chill prior to serving.

Makes 1 dozen

RAW

WHIPPED AVOCADO IN CUCUMBER CUPS

Visual appeal is important for most families, and this dish is a great feast for the eyes! It's fun, yet a very simple combination of foods that is also hydrating, satiating, and alkalizing. For additional protein, sprinkle in hemp seeds, or add essential fats by topping with pumpkin seeds.

INGREDIENTS

For the whipped avocado:

3 large Hass avocados

6 tablespoons lemon juice or 3 tablespoons lime juice

1 tablespoon onion powder

1 tablespoon garlic powder

1 teaspoon sea salt

For the cucumber cups:

2 large hothouse cucumbers

INSTRUCTIONS

For the whipped avocado, cut the avocados in half lengthwise. Then remove the pits. Scrape the avocado flesh into a medium mixing bowl, and save the skins. Using a fork, smash the avocado with all the remaining ingredients.

Using an immersion blender in a medium bowl, whip the avocado to a light and fluffy dip. You can use a basic blender if you do not have an immersion blender available. The avocado will blend up creamy, but it is much lighter when whipped.

For the cucumber cups, on a cutting board, divide each cucumber into 4 equal parts. (Cut in half and then cut those halves down again into quarters, creating sticks.)

Next, line up the avocado skins on the cutting board. Place 4 to 6 cucumber sticks in each with the tips coming together in the center of the skins. Scoop 4 to 6 ounces of whipped avocado into the center, filling each cup.

Chill until ready to serve.

Makes 6 servings

RAW

STUFFED BAKED BUTTERNUT SQUASH

♦

This is an easy recipe that combines some simple transitional cooked elements with great raw toppings.

INGREDIENTS

1 large butternut squash
Extra-virgin olive oil, for brushing

For the filling:

1½ cups walnuts

2 Roma tomatoes

½ cup diced red bell pepper

½ cup spinach

¼ cup extra-virgin olive oil

1 tablespoon dried Italian seasoning

1 tablespoon garlic powder

1 teaspoon onion powder

1 teaspoon sea salt

INSTRUCTIONS

Preheat the oven to 350°F.

Cut the butternut squash in half lengthwise. Remove the seeds. Place face-in, skin-side down, on a baking sheet. Brush with olive oil.

Bake in the oven for 25 to 30 minutes until a fork can easily pierce the flesh.

To make the filling, while you are waiting on the butternut squash, place all the filling ingredients in a food processor with the S-blade in place and pulse until a rough mixture has formed. It's important to pulse instead of turning on the processor fully in order to maintain the texture of the filling.

Remove the squash before the last 7 minutes of cook time, place the mixture on top, and place back in the oven for the remaining 7 minutes.

Makes 4 servings

CHEESY CAULIFLOWER

Cauliflower is fun as a side dish always, but with nutritional yeast, you can create a cheeselike flavor that really just enhances the flavor of the cauliflower itself. For this dish, you might try looking for orange cauliflower, as the color evokes the feeling of traditional cheese.

INGREDIENTS

4 cups cauliflower florets

For the sauce:

1 cup cashews or walnuts

¾ cup water

¼ cup nutritional yeast

2 tablespoons extra-virgin olive oil

2 tablespoons lemon juice

1 Roma tomato

1 teaspoon sea salt

INSTRUCTIONS

For the sauce, in a blender, combine all the sauce ingredients and blend on high speed. Transfer the sauce to a medium mixing bowl.

Add the cauliflower florets to the bowl and toss together well.

For dehydrating: Line a dehydration tray with a nonstick sheet. Scoop the cauliflower onto the tray. Dehydrate at 118°F for 3 hours.

For baking: Preheat the oven to 250°F. Scoop the cauliflower into a glass baking dish and press out flat. Then cook for 25 minutes.

Remove from cooking and serve warm. Refrigerate the leftovers for up to 3 days after cooking for use as a garnish in other dishes like salads or as another entrée/side dish option.

Makes 4 servings

RAW or TRANSITIONAL

MARINARA ZUCCHINI STICKS

These sticks are easy for little hands to grab! Colorful and flavorful, they enhance any meal. They can be prepared in the oven or the dehydrator depending on your available time. We love dehydrating because it makes the whole house smell like pizza!

INGREDIENTS

4 zucchini

For the marinara:

1 red bell pepper, stemmed, seeded, and cored

1 Roma tomato, cored

¼ cup extra-virgin olive oil

1 sun-dried tomato

¼ cup water

1 tablespoon nutritional yeast

1 teaspoon sea salt

1 teaspoon chile powder or dried Italian seasoning (optional)

INSTRUCTIONS

Prepare the zucchini by removing the ends. Using a mandoline, slice the squash lengthwise ¼ inch thick and place in a medium mixing bowl.

To make the marinara, in a basic blender, combine all the ingredients and blend well until a nice rich, thick paste is formed.

Pour this over the zucchini in the mixing bowl and carefully toss well until all the squash sticks are well coated.

Line a dehydration tray with a mesh screen and your choice of nonstick drying sheet. Line up each squash piece side by side but not overlapping. Place in the dehydrator at 118°F for 3 hours. Then gently remove the sticks from the nonstick drying sheet and place them directly on the screen to dry for 1 additional hour. Remove from the dehydrator and serve warm.

These can also be made in the oven: Preheat the oven to 350°F. Place the squash sticks seed-side up in a glass baking dish and bake for 15 minutes, leaving the door of the oven cracked. Remove from the oven and serve warm.

Makes 4 servings

RAW or TRANSITIONAL

RAWMESAN CHEESE

This sprinkle can punch up the flavor of any dish and makes a great Parmesan cheese substitute. Prepare it in the dehydrator for use all month long. I (Jenny) have seen this simple "cheese" totally turn around salads for resistant children—I call it the secret weapon of salads!

INGREDIENTS	INSTRUCTIONS
4 cups soaked shelled sunflower seeds, well rinsed*	Blend all the ingredients in a high-powered blender until well combined.
3 cups water	Prepare 2 dehydration trays by lining them with nonstick drying sheets. Evenly divide the mixture between the trays, spreading out using a spatula until thinly covering. Place in a dehydrator set at 118°F and dehydrate for 12 hours, or until completely dry. Crumble the mixture off the tray and store in a mason jar.
2 Roma tomatoes, cored	
½ cup nutritional yeast	
½ cup coconut aminos	
¼ cup lemon juice	
1 tablespoon sea salt	
	*To soak the seeds, add 4 cups sunflower seeds and 4½ cups water to a glass bowl. Let sit 4 hours and rinse well before use.

Makes 3 cups

RAW

Veggie Mama Idea for the Adventurous Family: Arts-and-Crafts Fair

Using fruits and vegetables as an activity is a great way to encourage exploration from an early age. Here is a chart of ideas you can use for your family with some basic tips on how to implement each. I recommend an Internet search for expanded ideas or visuals of how others have been able to modify these activities to suit their own family's needs.

TANGERINE PUMPKINS	Use peeled tangerines and small celery sticks to create mini-pumpkins.
BANANA GHOSTS	Cut bananas in half and use cloves to create eyes, noses, and mouths.
VEGETABLE TRAINS	Create trains using halved bell peppers for carts, and incorporate wheels using cucumber slices and toothpicks to hold in place.
CELERY AND CARROT BUILDINGS	Simple! Crisscross carrot and celery sticks to make Lincoln-log-style buildings.
MELON CUTOUTS	Cookie cutters can form cutouts from melons of all types when sliced thick—make hearts and stars and more!
GREEN GRAPE CATERPILLARS	Connect green grapes using toothpicks and then use wiggly eyes to brighten up your caterpillar and fresh cilantro for antennae.

Chapter 8

VEGGIE MAMA WHOLESOME SWEET TREATS AND DESSERTS

Fabulous and fruity, Veggie Mama desserts are by nature the epitome of "free" eating! That means these desserts are dairy-free, gluten-free, soy-free, and of course *guilt*-free. As a passionate Veggie Mama, you can read through our wholesome sweeteners list in the pantry section of Chapter 2 and decide which are best for your family as you create these delicious desserts.

One great benefit of desserts done the Veggie Mama way is that they are naturally chock-full of proteins and essential fatty acids—building blocks for life! Added health bonuses like antioxidants and even

carotenoids are present in these dessert favorites. In fact, most double as breakfasts or snacks too! These are the perfect treats to take along to birthday parties, as well, and will help you stand out from the crowd while at the same time providing something healthy. (Shhh . . . we won't tell if you don't!)

The secret is to create from the same list of ingredients you use as bases in the healthy kitchen you've created. You'll be pairing those simple foods with a healthy sweetener of choice and some upgraded cooking methods, like dehydrating or low-temperature baking, to keep these desserts low-glycemic.

Your healthful desserts will be at least 80 percent lower in sugar than the traditional counterparts out there.

If you have kids over nine who will be easing into new foods, you may wish to start with healthy desserts as your first transitional step in your Veggie Mama kitchen. Most kids develop a sweet tooth by the age of five, and this is a great opportunity to offer healthy dessert options and potentially rewrite any negative associations your children may have with natural foods. A common gripe with children transitioning their diets is that the food doesn't have as much flavor or doesn't taste good. Dessert is a simple tool to entice them to accept the idea that healthy food can be delicious and fun!

All the decisions you make in favor of fresh, healthy foods will add up to great benefits to your family's health and wellness, to be sure, but the decision to offer healthy desserts that are also low on the glycemic index (meaning they do not contain processed or refined sugars that boost—and lead to the overproduction of—insulin) is probably the greatest of all. Many of the health concerns we are facing in the world today are due to the overconsumption of sugars. The constant consumption of high-glycerin sugars and heavy carbohydrates can negatively impact children over their entire lives.

Research points to the conclusion that even though a body may "apparently" be able to process sugars without any of the warning signs of the most obvious insulin issue—diabetes—we may still be missing where the high-glycemic load is truly taking its toll: the brain!

The *Journal of Diabetes Science and Technology* has discussed through multiple studies first the hypothesis and then the eventual finding, in 2012, that the brain can be insulin resistant. The brain uses glucose too, and the issue here is that the overconsumption of sugar leaves plaque buildup. This is something that remains relatively unseen until the later part of life, when symptoms of Alzheimer's and dementia become obvious; however, all along from birth until this time, the consumption of sugar has been playing a role in what is now referred to as *type 3 diabetes*.

The point here is to outline the importance of taking a stand for your child's well-being and encourage you to be steadfast in creating these health opportunities for your family. In many seen and unseen ways, you are quietly benefiting your family's legacy of health. Just how diet affects your children may not be obvious until they are fully grown or even in their senior years, as evidenced by the current findings on sugar and the brain. Research also suggests that we are influencing the genetic code that is passed down generation after generation with our food choices, as well as establishing routines around food that will be shared for years to come. Your Veggie Mama commitment through your daily decisions with respect to food may, in fact, be rewriting and architecting the future of your family lineage.

Veggie Mama Idea for the Adventurous Family: Family Dessert Potluck

When we think of celebrations, we tend to think of something sweet! To make these sweet moments even more impactful with your family, you may institute a commemorative potluck. Each family member brings a dessert, and you can enjoy them all as a group. Children can be hands-on with making age-appropriate dessert items or partner with older siblings to create more complex recipes for your next celebration! Healthy desserts are typically high in essential nutrients, so you might consider adding to the fun and implementing a "backward day" starting with desserts first! This is a crowd-pleaser, for sure!

NO-BAKE CARROT CAKE

This is a perfect Veggie Mama example of how you can create an effortless dessert by combining some simple ingredients in the food processor! Carrots made into a cake have a different attraction for kids as well, so this is an easy recipe to help your children learn to love these root vegetables.

INGREDIENTS

For the crust:

½ cup coconut shreds

2 cups coconut or almond flour

½ cup pitted dates

1 teaspoon sea salt

For the cake:

2 cups shredded carrots

½ cup raisins

½ cup coconut or almond flour

1 tablespoon ground cinnamon

1 teaspoon sea salt

INSTRUCTIONS

For the crust, in a food processor with the S-blade attachment in place, first process down the coconut shreds and flour of choice. Then add the dates and sea salt and process until a dough ball forms.

Remove the crust and chill prior to use.

For the cake, in the food processor with the S-blade attachment still in place, process the carrots for 30 seconds until a carrot meal has formed.

Add in the raisins, flour, cinnamon, and salt and process until a light, fluffy mix has formed.

Now press the crust into a spring-form 8-inch pie pan or into individual pie pans.

Top the crust evenly with the cake mixture.

Chill the cake prior to serving. This cake is delicious right away . . . but *incredible* after it sits for 1 to 2 days!

Makes 8 individual cakes or one 8-inch cake | RAW

CHOCOLATE CHIA PUDDING

This is an easy make-ahead recipe that you can use for dessert parfaits all week long. In a group setting, participants can have fun adding their own toppings. Also, if you freeze this recipe, it quickly becomes a soft gelato!

INGREDIENTS	INSTRUCTIONS
6 bananas	Blend all ingredients well in a high-powered blender.
⅓ cup raw coconut nectar	
⅓ cup raw cacao	Chill and let set. The chia seeds will thicken the mixture after 10 to 20 minutes.
2 cups coconut water (or regular water)	
2 tablespoons chia seeds	Serve chilled or freeze for go-to gelato.
2 tablespoons coconut oil	
1 teaspoon sea salt	

Makes 4 cups

RAW

BANANA BREAD

This gluten-free loaf is a great staple for any Veggie Mama kitchen! This recipe provides an excellent source of potassium, while at the same time serving as a versatile snack that can be packed in a lunch or enjoyed on its own as a breakfast or dessert.

INGREDIENTS

2 cups chopped bananas

2 tablespoons ground cinnamon

1 teaspoon sea salt

1 teaspoon vanilla paste

4 cups gluten-free flour mix

¼ cup ground golden flaxseeds

INSTRUCTIONS

Preheat the oven to 350°F.

In a basic blender, blend the banana, cinnamon, salt, and vanilla paste together until a thick puree is formed.

Transfer the puree to a medium mixing bowl and fold in the gluten-free flour and flaxseeds. Stir the mixture well and then transfer to a loaf pan for baking.

Bake for 25 minutes until a cakelike texture has formed. Insert in a toothpick at the center to be sure no batter remains.

Remove from the oven and let cool, transfer to a cutting board, and cut into desired serving sizes.

Makes 1 loaf

RAW COOKIE DOUGH

Here it is: a Veggie Mama–friendly recipe that is completely delicious and an excellent raw preparation! This mixture can be made in advance and frozen for use throughout the entire month, pressed into cookies, enjoyed by the spoonful, or made into a great crust, like in some of our frozen Veggie Mama pies.

INGREDIENTS	INSTRUCTIONS
½ cup coconut shreds	In a blender, pulse the coconut shreds down into a meal.
4 cups almond flour	
½ cup coconut nectar	Transfer the coconut meal to the food processor with the S-blade attachment in place and add all the other cookie dough ingredients. Process until a dough ball forms.
1 tablespoon vanilla paste	
1 teaspoon sea salt	
	Although this is a shelf-stable combination of ingredients, we recommend refrigerating the mix or freezing it for use throughout the month.

Makes 4 1/2 cups   RAW

SUMMER PROTEIN POPS

When you freeze a nice rich blend of plant-powered protein, fruits, and nut or seed mylk, you create a much healthier version of an ice-cream pop that can be universally enjoyed as a sweet treat and a functional food. We recommend that you look for a pop tray that has at least six molds in it so that you can easily freeze the whole batch at once.

INGREDIENTS	INSTRUCTIONS
3 cups nut or seed mylk	In a blender, combine the mylk, 2½ cups of the chopped mango, and the bananas, protein, sweetener, and coconut oil on high speed until well combined.
3 cups chopped mango, strawberry, or pineapple (fresh or frozen)	
2 bananas	Dice the remanding ½ cup mango and evenly divide among 6 pop molds.
3 servings plant-based protein (either pea or brown rice, we recommend using a vanilla flavor, or unsweetened)	Pour the pop mixture evenly into the pop molds.
2 tablespoons raw sweetener of choice	Freeze for 8 hours, until well set, and then remove from the pop mold. Enjoy!
2 tablespoons coconut oil	

Makes 6 medium pops | RAW

ALYSA'S BLUEBERRY PIE

I (Jenny) was working with my then-two-year-old daughter in the kitchen, playing with blueberries, and this concoction emerged. Luckily, our combination worked out and this rich and creamy frozen pie was born. This recipe is best, in our opinion, as an individual portion but can also be prepared as a large pie for celebrations and the like.

INGREDIENTS	INSTRUCTIONS
For the crust: 2 cups Raw Cookie Dough (page 170) **For the pie filling:** ⅔ cup water ⅓ cup coconut nectar 1 cup frozen blueberries 1½ cups sprouted cashews* 1 tablespoon vanilla paste 1 teaspoon sea salt	For the crust, line the bottom of either your pie pan or individual molds with the Raw Cookie Dough crust and press to ½ inch thick. For the pie filling, in a blender, combine all the pie ingredients, loading in the liquids first for best results, and blend until rich and creamy. Pour the pie mixture over the crust. Freeze for 6 hours before serving. *Optional:* Sprinkle with additional Raw Cookie Dough crust pieces for a delicious topping! *To sprout, cover with water and let sit for 4 to 6 hours prior to use. Rinse well and then pat dry before incorporating into the recipe.

Makes 8 to 10 servings

RAW

NUT-FREE BROWNIES

This is a nut-free preparation that uses oat flour as the base, providing some variety for your menus and also ensuring you are rotating ingredients so that your overall food consumption is well balanced.

INGREDIENTS

For the frosting:

1 large Hass avocado

⅓ cup raw cacao

⅓ cup coconut nectar or pitted dates

1 tablespoon coconut oil

1 teaspoon ground cinnamon

1 teaspoon sea salt

½ cup water

For the brownies:

2 cups gluten-free oat flour

½ cup raw cacao

½ cup pitted dates

2 tablespoons coconut oil

1 teaspoon sea salt

INSTRUCTIONS

For the frosting, in a blender, blend all the frosting ingredients on high speed until well combined, rich, and creamy. Refrigerate until ready to use.

For the brownies, in a food processor with the S-blade attachment in place, combine all the brownie ingredients and process until a dough ball has formed.

Press the brownie dough evenly into an 8-inch square baking dish.

Top with the frosting mix. Spread evenly.

Chill, then cut into serving portions and chill for an additional hour in the refrigerator before serving. Once the mix has initially chilled, it may be left out and will still hold for up to 4 hours.

Makes 8 to 10 servings   RAW

CASHEW CHOCOLATE SWEETS

These are simple to prepare and may be formed into all different types of shapes and varying sizes. This recipe uses raw cacao, which is higher in minerals like magnesium, for growing healthy bones, than roasted cocoa powder.

INGREDIENTS	INSTRUCTIONS
2 cups raw cashews	In a food processor with the S-blade attachment in place, grind the cashews into a meal.
½ cup coconut flakes	
⅓ cup raw cacao	Add the coconut flakes, cacao, cinnamon, and sea salt, and pulse until a coarse mix is formed.
1 tablespoon ground cinnamon	
1 teaspoon sea salt	
⅓ cup raw agave nectar or coconut nectar	Add the raw agave through the feed tube on the food processor while running the machine. A dough ball will form.
	Stop the machine and remove the dough ball, transferring it onto a silicone sheet or cutting board lined with plastic wrap.
	Form and mold into desired shapes and sizes. This is a shelf-stable mixture, so it does not need to be refrigerated.
	Optional: Top with—or roll shapes in—more coconut flakes, cacao nibs, or other superfoods (like hemp seeds) for additional nutritional components and flavors.

Makes 4 cups dough | RAW

MINI APPLE COBBLERS

Small cobblers are a fun and inviting dessert that can be enjoyed as a sweet surprise and are a great addition to birthday parties and celebrations.

INGREDIENTS

For the apple cobbler filling:

6 apples, cored

¼ cup raw coconut nectar or 4 drops stevia

1 tablespoon ground cinnamon

2 teaspoons pumpkin pie spice

1 teaspoon sea salt

For the topping:

½ cup raw walnuts or pecan pieces

1 teaspoon ground cinnamon

1 pinch sea salt

For the crust:

2 cups Simple Crust (page 180)

INSTRUCTIONS

For the cobbler filling, cut the apples into quarters and then cut into thin slices ¼ inch thick. You may elect to do this in a food processor with the slicing blade in place or on a mandoline.

In a medium mixing bowl, whisk the sweetener and all the spices together until well combined. Transfer the apple slices to the bowl. Toss until they are well coated in the spices.

Let sit until ready to use.

For the topping, in your choice of blender, coffee grinder, or food processor, grind the topping ingredients until a meal is formed to sprinkle over the top of the cobbler. Be sure not to overprocess so that the mixture does not become thick or buttery but rather stays light and fluffy.

For the crust, fill 8 small ramekins with approximately 2 tablespoons Simple Crust mixture each. Lightly wet your fingers and press the dough into the bottom of the ramekin evenly.

INSTRUCTIONS, CONT'D.

Then fill the ramekins evenly with the apple cobbler filling mixture.

Finally, sprinkle each with the topping mixture.

For finishing these cobblers, you have three options:

1. Enjoy in the spring and summer as is;

2. Dehydrate in a dehydrator at 118°F for 4 hours for a soft and warm cobbler; or

3. Bake at 300°F for 10 minutes.

You can decide based on time and resources which option is the best fit for you!

Makes 8 mini cobblers

RAW or TRANSITIONAL

SIMPLE CRUST

This crust has served as a no-fuss four-ingredient base for a number of delicious sweet treats, including dessert bars, cookies, cakes, and cobblers. You can whip up three batches and freeze two of the three for easy recipe preparation on a Veggie Mama whim! Just knowing this crust is available and at the ready is enough to set your healthy sweet tooth at ease.

INGREDIENTS	INSTRUCTIONS
3 cups raw pecans or walnut pieces*	In the food processor with the S-blade attachment in place, grind the nuts of choice into a meal.
1 tablespoon ground cinnamon	
1 teaspoon sea salt	Add the cinnamon, salt, and vanilla paste, and lightly pulse until combined.
1 tablespoon vanilla paste (optional)	
⅓ cup raw coconut nectar, raw honey, or raw agave nectar**	Turn on the food processor and add the sweetener through the feed tube while the blade is spinning. A dough ball will begin to form. Stop the processor once well combined and the mixture is sticking to itself.
	Remove the mixture for use in a number of recipes. Alternatively, the dough can be simply rolled in a number of spices and superfoods to create simple grab-and-go energy snacks!
	*For nut-allergic children, pumpkin seeds may be used. Pumpkin seeds do not contain as much oil, so we recommend purchasing raw unsalted pumpkin seeds out of the shell, and you may need to use more in the recipe for the same result. Try adding 2 additional tablespoons at a time until you achieve a soft yet firm texture that holds body.
	**You may also use stevia in this crust for a lower-glycemic dessert. In order to do so, you will want to blend together 4 to 6 drops liquid stevia, 2 tablespoons raw almond butter, and ¼ cup water to create a viscous liquid to add to the mixture and help bind the ingredients in the dough together.

Makes 2 cups dough | RAW

EASY COOKIES

These cookies are perfect for a cookie bar at a children's party and are featured in the Party-Food Favors (page 217). They are equally enjoyable for all members of the family and can be adapted to suit any palate. We recommend making two batches at a time, as they will go fast!

INGREDIENTS

3 cups almond meal

1 cup coconut flour or oat flour

1 teaspoon sea salt

⅓ cup almond butter

¼ cup raw sweetener of choice

Optional flavor add-ins:

⅓ cup raw cacao powder

⅓ cup raw carob powder

⅓ cup coconut flakes

⅓ cup chopped dried apricot

¼ cup raw cacao nibs

2 tablespoons hemp seeds

INSTRUCTIONS

In a large mixing bowl, combine the almond meal, flour of choice, and sea salt. Whisk the ingredients together.

Add in any dry flavor options you'd like and whisk together one more time.

Then add in the almond butter and sweetener of choice and knead until a well-combined dough is formed.

Transfer the dough to a silicone sheet or a cutting board lined with plastic wrap. Press out and cut into desired shapes, or roll into balls.

Then dehydrate at 118°F for 2 hours. You may also elect to enjoy the cookies raw! Or you may wish to bake them at 250°F for 10 minutes. Once complete, place on a cake stand on your counter so you can enjoy these healthy sweet treats all week long.

Makes 12 to 16 cookies

RAW or TRANSITIONAL

EASY DESSERT SAUCES

For some simple toppings over fresh fruit or for an easy anytime dessert, try these four-ingredient sauces!

CACAO SAUCE:

1 cup raw coconut nectar

¼ to ⅓ cup raw cacao (the more you add, the richer the flavor)

1 tablespoon raw coconut oil

1 pinch sea salt

BERRY PUREE:

1 cup sliced strawberries

1 cup raspberries

1 teaspoon coconut nectar

1 pinch sea salt

In a basic blender, blend the ingredients of your chosen recipe until well combined.

The Cacao Sauce does not need to be refrigerated and can be transferred to a glass storage jar or a squeeze bottle for easy serving.

The Berry Puree should be transferred to an airtight bottle stored in the refrigerator for up to 1 week's enjoyment.

♥ ♥ ♥

Chapter 9

VEGGIE MAMA "I'M HUNGRY" GO-TO SNACKS AND NOURISHING PALATE PLEASERS

Snacks represent a positive and uplifting opportunity for your family if done right. Many families tend to tuck all the fresh foods in their house away in the refrigerator and then place all the packaged ones out on the counter. If you are a family transitioning your diet, this could be a pattern that is hard to overcome. Many of our Veggie Mama snacks are designed to leave out in plain sight, so adults and kids alike can snack on fresh foods that fuel them for success.

You can easily leave an array of snacks on the counter, buffet-style. The "afternoon snack buffet" was conceived when my (Jenny's) kids began school. We were always coming home hungry and in a hurry, so having these foods ready and waiting was a welcome relief and added some relaxation to everyone's day. This is the type of food security veggie kids are happy to find. It's possible your kids may not be around healthy vegan snacks all day, other than what is packed for them. Coming home to a full counter of treats is a daily ritual that makes this lifestyle choice fun and special! Of course, each member of your family will have his or her own favorites, but we try to add in one new selection each week or simply modify the fruits and vegetables to consistently develop the tastes of growing children.

NUT BUTTER BITES

These can be made with either a nut butter or a seed butter and are a fast, simple creation that kids love to make too! This is a great hands-on learning exercise for young kids especially, and can be modified to fit your own family's needs.

INGREDIENTS	INSTRUCTIONS
For the base:	For the base, in a food processor with the S-blade attachment in place, process all the base ingredients until well combined.
3 cups nut or seed butter of choice	
½ cup coconut, almond, or gluten-free oat flour	
½ cup liquid sweetener of choice	Pulse in any additional options until well integrated into the mix.
2 tablespoons ground cinnamon	
1 teaspoon sea salt	Roll out the dough into a long, roundish shape. Cut into 18 equal portions.
Optional add-ins:	Make different designs on the bites. either with the back of a fork or other stamplike imprint, as you desire.
¼ cup hemp seeds	
¼ cup cacao nibs	
½ cup raisins	

Makes 18 bites | RAW

BERRIES WITH HEMP BUTTER

Hemp butter is fast and simple to make yourself, or you can purchase premade. The butter itself is shelf-stable, so when you add it to fresh berries for your snack display, it will not need additional refrigeration as long as the berries are whole. However, we do recommend you refrigerate any uneaten berries for the next day once they are spread with the hemp butter. (When the two ingredients sit together for more than 4 hours, the interaction between the oil and the fruit can cause the fruit to break down, so refrigeration is needed.) This dish is naturally high in antioxidants and healthy omega fatty acids.

INGREDIENTS	INSTRUCTIONS
For the butter: 16 ounces hemp seeds 2 tablespoons water 1 tablespoon coconut oil 1 teaspoon sea salt **For the snack dish:** Up to 16 large strawberries, depending on the size of your family	For the butter, in a blender, preferably with a small canister,* combine all the butter ingredients and blend until a rich, thick, and creamy spread is formed. For the snack dish, before serving, wash the strawberries well and dry off. Spread 1 to 2 teaspoons butter on the berries and serve on a tray butter-side up! Add toothpicks for smaller fingers to more easily grab. *You can also blend using a food processor with the S-blade attachment in place, but the final mixture will not be as creamy.

Makes up to 16 servings | RAW

DYLAN'S BUCKWHEAT CRISPS

As I (Jenny) have mentioned, I had to work around numerous allergies with my son, Dylan. My aim became to make a crunchy, delicious, gluten-, soy-, and of course dairy-free cracker. This has become a well-loved family favorite! These crackers are also fully dehydrated, so they have great shelf life. You can make a large batch and store in the pantry indefinitely.

INGREDIENTS	INSTRUCTIONS
2 cups water	In a blender, blend the water, Roma tomato, garlic, salt, and chile powder until well combined.
1 Roma tomato, cored	
1 clove garlic	
1 teaspoon sea salt	Add in the buckwheat groats and chia seeds and blend well until a thick paste has formed.
1 teaspoon chile powder	
4 cups buckwheat groats	
½ cup ground chia seeds	Transfer the mixture to lined dehydrator trays, forming 4-inch-diameter rounds, ¼ inch thick.
	Dehydrate at 118°F for up to 24 hours, until the crackers are crunchy.
	Alternatively, you can transfer in the same manner to a cookie sheet and bake the crackers at 250°F for up to 2 hours.
	These crackers can be stored in an airtight container and pair nicely with the Tahini Cheese Spread on page 191 for an afternoon snack!

Makes 16 crisps

RAW or TRANSITIONAL

SWEET PUMPKIN BUTTER SPREAD

When in season, pumpkins are a great colorful source of iron and potassium. This sweet spread can be used as a snack or even a savory dessert item.

INGREDIENTS

1½ cups cubed pumpkin

2 tablespoons raw coconut nectar

2 tablespoons coconut butter or almond butter

1 tablespoon ground cinnamon

1 teaspoon sea salt

Water as needed

INSTRUCTIONS

Blend all the ingredients well in a high-powered blender, adding water as necessary to turn the blades (no more than ¼ cup water should be needed), until a nice, thick butter forms.

Remove the mixture from the blender and refrigerate for up to 7 days.

Makes 2 cups

RAW

PUMPKIN SEED BARS

Pumpkin seeds are an easy high-protein addition to any snack, and because this recipe is so simple, we recommend including it in your weekly food preparations as an easy go-to for your child's lunch box!

INGREDIENTS	INSTRUCTIONS
4 cups pumpkin seeds	In a food processor with the S-blade attachment in place, combine all the ingredients and process until a thick dough is formed.
1½ cups soaked, dried Mission figs	
2 tablespoons ground cinnamon	
1 teaspoon sea salt	
	Press the dough into an 8 × 8-inch square on a covered cutting board.
	Cut into 2 × 2-inch squares.
	Refrigerate to keep the flavor fresh.

Makes 16 bars | RAW

TAHINI CHEESE SPREAD

This favorite at my (Jenny's) 118 Degrees restaurant is included here because it's a simple Veggie Mama recipe to ensure some great minerals, including iron and calcium, and B vitamins are found in your family meal. Naturally, this spread is a great energy booster as an afternoon snack as well! This "cheese" sits well out of the refrigerator for up to 4 hours, so it can be placed on a snack buffet or in a grab-and-go lunch.

INGREDIENTS	INSTRUCTIONS
½ cup lemon juice	In a food processor with the S-blade attachment in place, process the lemon juice, garlic, cilantro, green onions, and salt.
2 cloves garlic	
⅓ cup fresh cilantro leaves	
½ cup chopped green onions	Add the tahini through the feed tube while the machine is running and continue processing until a thick paste forms.
1 tablespoon sea salt	
2 cups tahini paste	Refrigerate for up to 10 days.

Makes 3 cups

RAW

NUT-FREE TRAIL MIX

❖

This recipe is simple to prepare and is another way to get more healthy fats into your child's snack time.

INGREDIENTS	INSTRUCTIONS
2 cups raw sunflower seeds	Preheat the oven to 200°F.
2 cups raw pumpkin seeds	In a large mixing bowl, toss all the ingredients together until the seeds are well coated in sweetener.
2 cups sliced dried apricots	
⅓ cup hemp seeds	Transfer the mixture to a lined baking dish or tray and place in the oven for 20 minutes, or until dry to the touch.
¼ cup raw liquid sweetener of choice	
1½ teaspoons coconut oil	
1 teaspoon sea salt	Alternatively, try dehydrating: Cover a dehydrator tray with parchment paper and transfer the mixture to the tray. Dehydrate at 118°F for 4 hours, or until dry to the touch.
	Store in an airtight container until ready to eat.

Makes 6 cups | RAW

TRAIL MIX COOKIES

A secondary use for leftover trail mix is to integrate it into this simple cookie recipe, which can be enjoyed either lightly baked or raw.

INGREDIENTS	INSTRUCTIONS
For the base: 1 cup buckwheat flour ½ cup pumpkin seed meal ¼ cup raw liquid sweetener of choice 1 tablespoon ground cinnamon 1 teaspoon sea salt **For the topping:** ½ cup Nut-Free Trail Mix (page 192)	For the base, in a food processor with the S-blade attachment in place, combine all the base cookie ingredients and process until a dough is formed. Transfer the mixture to a cutting board and press into individual 2-inch round cookies. For the topping, press the trail mix into the cookies. If desired, bake at 250°F for 12 minutes or enjoy completely raw.

Makes 12 small cookies

RAW

MANGO VANILLA CUSTARD

A colorful and delicious combination of foods, this dish makes for a great eye-catching display at your snack station and is easy to prepare in advance and store in the refrigerator until ready to use.

INGREDIENTS	INSTRUCTIONS
For the vanilla custard: 1 cup macadamia nuts or cashews ⅓ cup coconut shreds ⅓ cup water ⅓ cup sweetener of choice 1 tablespoon vanilla paste 1 teaspoon sea salt **For the mango topping:** 1 cup chopped frozen mango 2 tablespoons orange juice	For the custard, in a blender, combine all the custard ingredients and blend well on high speed until a rich, creamy custard has formed. Refrigerate until ready to use. For the mango topping, in the same blender without washing, blend the mango and orange juice on high speed until well combined. Layer equal parts of the mixture in 6 mason jars or small cups and refrigerate until ready to eat.

Makes six 4-ounce servings

RAW

BROCCOLI POPPERS

Oh my! These are every Veggie Mama's dream! There are two marinade flavors featured here, for easy integration into your snack lineup. Both versions offer a great source of essential fatty acids and, of course, a healthy dose of broccoli!

INGREDIENTS	INSTRUCTIONS
6 cups broccoli florets	In a large mixing bowl, separate the florets until each is about 1 inch in diameter on the top.
For the pesto walnut marinade:	For the marinade, in a blender, combine the ingredients for the marinade of choice and blend until rich and creamy.
1 cup walnut pieces	
½ cup fresh basil leaves	
⅓ cup extra-virgin olive oil	Toss the marinade over the florets, ensuring they are well coated.
2 cloves garlic	
1 tablespoon sea salt	You can either dehydrate these poppers or bake them at a low temperature in the oven.
For the cheesy marinade:	*For dehydrating:* Line 4 dehydration trays and cover evenly with the marinated broccoli florets. Dehydrate at 118°F for 14 hours, until crunchy. We recommend rotating the florets after 6 hours for more even drying.
¾ cup tahini paste	
⅓ cup chopped tomato	
¼ cup nutritional yeast	
1 clove garlic	
½ cup water	*For baking:* Preheat the oven to 250°F. Line 2 baking trays and evenly divide the poppers between the trays. Bake for 25 minutes, then crack the door and bake for an additional 7 minutes. If you have a convection oven, this feature is recommended for this recipe.
1 tablespoon sea salt	

Remove the poppers, let cool, and store in an airtight container if completely dry. If they still contain any moisture, refrigerate until serving.

Makes 6 cups

EASY KALE CHIPS

Kale chips are a fun approach to getting this healthy vegetable into your child's meal rotation. They are light and crispy, as well as flavorful!

INGREDIENTS	INSTRUCTIONS

For the marinade:

½ cup tahini paste

½ cup chopped tomato

⅓ cup diced red bell pepper

2 tablespoons nutritional yeast

2 tablespoons lemon juice

1 clove garlic

1 tablespoon sea salt

¾ cup water

For the chips:

16 cups cleaned kale leaves, stems removed

For the marinade, in a blender, blend all the marinade ingredients on high speed until well combined.

For the chips, place the kale leaves in a large mixing bowl. Check to see that they are 3 × 3 inches in size, roughly. Pull apart any larger leaves.

Coat the leaves with the marinade and toss together well.

You can either dehydrate these chips or bake them at a low temperature in the oven.

For dehydrating: Line 6 dehydration trays and top evenly with the kale leaves. Dehydrate at 118°F for 12 to 14 hours, until completely dry and crunchy. You may want to flip them after about 6 hours to shorten the dehydrating time.

For baking: Preheat the oven to 250°F. Line 2 baking trays with foil and divide the kale leaves evenly between the trays, making sure they do not overlap. Bake for 35 minutes. Be sure to check them at 25 and 30 minutes. Each head of kale has a different level of moisture, so your baking time may not be exact. (You want them dry but not burned.)

Remove and store in an airtight container until ready to use.

Serves 5 cups

RAW or TRANSITIONAL

Chapter 10

VEGGIE MAMA ADVENTURES IN SPROUTED AND FERMENTED FOODS

Beginning with sprouted and fermented foods is very simple. Our family-favorite sprout mix includes buckwheat, quinoa, lentils, and peas. We simply soak the buckwheat and quinoa overnight in water (enough to cover the top of the grain in the bowl) and do the same with the legumes in another bowl, preparing all the sprouts for use later in the week. Finally, we rinse the sprouts and toss them together before enjoying.

Another great fermented option, raw sauerkraut, is increasingly easy to find at the store, so for a beneficial shortcut, you can toss your sprout mix or use it along with the sauerkraut for a protein-rich probiotic topping to your salads, snacks, and soups!

Sprouted Foods

Sprouts are the beginning of all life for nuts, seeds, grains, and legumes. For many families, sprouting can be a great lesson on the life cycle of plants, while at the same time offering some fun textures and tastes to play with in the kitchen. Sprouting is a lot like indoor gardening and can be done year-round.

Kids in particular benefit from the added enzymes and minerals in sprouts as they develop strong bones and skeletal systems. Adults enjoying sprouts generally report enhanced digestion and optimized energy. Sprouting is very simple and really can be a great opportunity for learning and growth. In some recipes, we recommend using "sprouted" grains and seeds for better digestion. While this is optimal, it's not "necessary," always. We highly recommend exploring sprouting in your own kitchen!

Use this chart to implement interactive sprouting activities in your own kitchen. Choose among 1-, 3-, and 5-day sprouts so that you can have varying sprout combinations to add to salads and wraps or enjoy alone!

1-DAY SPROUTS (12 HOURS)	3-DAY SPROUTS	5-DAY SPROUTS
Quinoa	Flaxseeds	Broccoli
Garbanzo beans	Watermelon seeds	Mung bean

A dear friend of mine (Jenny's), "sprout-man" Steve Meyerowitz, taught me that sprouting could be a way of life. Harvesting sprouts is easy and somewhat like having a science experiment in the kitchen every day. Steve's encouragement led me to try sprouts first for my own enjoyment and then for my family's. Steve raised three children with sprouts and wheatgrass constantly growing in his kitchen. I have the great honor of working with his super-healthy now-adult children, and I can see what a lifetime of sprouts looks like!

Veggie Mama Idea for the Adventurous Family: Sprouting Science Experiments

Sprouts contain all the essence of the entire life of the plant in one single sprouted seed. Over the summer, try sprouting many different seeds with your family. The visual of seeing a fresh seed sprout is a powerful tool for teaching about the energetics of foods and the possibilities of a vibrant lifestyle through food. Visit sproutman.com to get ideas on going in depth with sprouting and to order seeds. If you set up this exercise as a science experiment, you can encourage your kids to track the progress of the sprout, taste it at different stages, and record their findings in a sprout science log!

QUINOA KIDNEY-BEAN SPROUTED VEGGIE PATTY

— ❧ —

This patty combines the best of raw-foods nutrition with some high-mineral foods like kidney beans that are not as predominant in a vegan diet because many people are not well versed in preparing different entrées with them. When we started experimenting with kidney beans as a base for a delicious vegetable patty, we were pleasantly surprised by the subtle, sweet flavor of the final product. Pair this with the Sprouted-Kamut Bread (page 205) or the Easy Wraps (page 146) for a tasty combination. If you have some Tahini Sauce (page 141) lying around, you can dip the patties for another simple snack!

INGREDIENTS

4 cups kidney beans

2 cups sprouted sunflower seeds*

2 cups sprouted quinoa

1 cup almond meal (can be substituted with oat flour for nut allergies)

¼ cup ground golden flaxseeds

1 tablespoon dried Italian seasoning

1 tablespoon garlic powder

1 tablespoon onion powder

1 teaspoon sea salt

⅓ cup water

INSTRUCTIONS

In a food processor with the S-blade attachment in place, process the kidney beans, sunflower seeds, and quinoa until a coarse meal is formed.

Add the almond meal, ground flaxseeds, and all the seasonings and pulse to combine the ingredients.

While the food processor is on, add the water through the feed tube in the top and process for 30 to 40 seconds, until a thick mixture is formed.

Line a dehydration tray with Teflex or silicone. Scoop out the patty mixture and press down into the desired shape and size on the tray.

Dehydrate at 118°F for 4 hours, or until the patty is dry to the touch on the outside.

If you do not yet have a dehydrator, you can still prepare this mixture and use it fresh as a fun and simple filling for wraps and handheld snacks. The mixture will keep fresh for up to 5 days in the refrigerator.

*Begin sprouting by soaking the shelled seeds in water for 6 hours. Then rinse prior to using. They will not yet be growing a tail, but they will have released the "enzyme inhibitor" present in all nuts and seeds, beginning the process of sprouting. This is the same course all seeds take prior to growing into a sprout and eventually a full-size plant!

Makes 6 patties	RAW

SPROUTED LENTIL SPREAD

Lentils are a great source of plant-based protein, and this fresh take on bean dip will be a pleasant add-on for any Veggie Mama hoping to get more protein into her child's diet. You can use this as a dip for crackers or vegetables or include it as a filling in tacos or on tostadas as a rich layer of flavorful nutrition.

INGREDIENTS

½ cup water

3 tablespoons extra-virgin olive oil

1 tablespoon raw sweetener of choice

1 Roma tomato, cored and chopped

1 clove garlic

1 tablespoon onion powder

1 tablespoon nutritional yeast

1 teaspoon sea salt

½ cup walnuts

1 cup sprouted lentils*

INSTRUCTIONS

In a blender, combine all the ingredients, adding in the liquids first, followed by the tomato and spices, and then the heavier nuts and lentils.

Blend the mixture on high speed until a rich, creamy sauce is formed. Remove the sauce from the blender and refrigerate until ready to use.

This spread is good for up to 5 days in the refrigerator.

*You can sprout the lentils overnight the evening before preparing this spread by covering ⅔ cup dried lentils in water with an additional inch of water over the top to allow for expansion of the lentils as they soak and sprout. Rinse them well in the morning, and a tail should be coming off of them at this point, signifying they are ready to use.

Makes 2 cups

RAW

SPROUTED-KAMUT BREAD

Sprouted kamut is an ancient grain that was originally discovered in an Egyptian tomb. It is a relative of wheat, so the grain still contains gluten. However, the gluten is in trace amounts compared to modern hybridized wheat. This grain is a nice Veggie Mama option for adding proteins to the diet but still leaving out processed breads. This is a flatbread prepared in the dehydrator. Once prepared, this bread will last for up to 21 days in the refrigerator. We have also provided some options for add-ins to modify the flavor to suit your own preferences.

INGREDIENTS	INSTRUCTIONS

For the bread:

6 cups sprouted kamut*

2 cloves garlic

¼ cup extra-virgin olive oil

1 teaspoon sea salt

⅓ cup water (as needed)

Flavor add-ins:

⅓ cup pitted kalamata olives

½ cup sun-dried tomatoes

⅓ cup fresh basil leaves

*Begin sprouting by placing the kamut in a midsize bowl and covering with water up to one inch over the top of the grains. You can leave the bowl out on your counter, but cover with a breathable material such as cheesecloth or plastic wrap with holes poked through. After 12 hours, rinse the grains well and return to the bowl. Continue to let the kamut sit out until it is soft and begins to grow a tail, rinsing every 12 hours. (In most climates, this should happen between days two and three.) Refrigerate the kamut for up to five days, until you're ready to use it. Rinse well before using in a recipe.

For the bread, in a food processor with the S-blade attachment in place, combine the kamut, garlic, oil, salt, and any desired add-ins. Process until a thick dough has formed. As needed, add the water through the feed tube to create a looser dough if the S-blade begins to stick.

Cover 2 dehydration trays with plastic film. Set the dehydrator at 118°F.

Transfer the dough to the dehydrator trays, dividing evenly, and press down firmly to create flatbread about ½ inch thick.

Place in the dehydrator for 2 hours, after which the top of the bread should be dry to the touch. Flip the bread over onto 2 new trays that are not lined, and dehydrate for an additional 2 to 3 hours, or until completely dry to the touch yet soft in the center.

Remove from the dehydrator and let cool. Refrigerate until ready to use.

Makes 2 trays, or 12 pieces of bread | RAW

SPROUTED-BUCKWHEAT SNACK MIX

Sprouted buckwheat, once dehydrated or baked at a low temperature, is a nice crunchy, gluten-free alternative to traditional crackers or cereals. Once dried, this snack will last indefinitely in an airtight container, so the preplanning Veggie Mama can use this as a go-to base recipe to make one time per month!

INGREDIENTS

4 cups spouted buckwheat*

1 cup soaked almonds or soaked pumpkin seeds

¼ cup soaked raisins

½ cup sun-dried tomatoes

¼ cup water

2 tablespoons extra-virgin olive oil

2 tablespoons onion powder

2 tablespoons garlic powder

1 tablespoon finely ground sea salt

INSTRUCTIONS

In a medium mixing bowl, rinse the buckwheat and your choice of almonds or pumpkin seeds well. Then add the raisins to the mix and let sit.

In a blender, blend the sun-dried tomatoes, water, olive oil, garlic and onion powders, and sea salt to a thick paste.

Add this blend to the bowl. Then toss the entire mixture together, making sure it is all well coated.

For dehydrating: Transfer the mixture to 2 dehydration trays lined with nonstick sheets. Dehydrate at 118°F for 6 hours.

For baking: Preheat the oven to 250°F and transfer the mixture to a cookie sheet lined with foil. Bake for 25 minutes, until dry and crunchy.

*To sprout buckwheat, simply soak in water overnight. Be sure to fill up the container with an extra inch of water above the buckwheat to allow for expansion. Rinse the buckwheat after 12 hours of soaking and use immediately or refrigerate for up to 3 days. Be sure to rinse the buckwheat once a day and prior to use.

Makes 8 cups

RAW or TRANSITIONAL

Fermented Foods

Fermentation is a process of nurturing cultured vegetables to a more enzyme-rich nutrient state by adding beneficial probiotics to the mix and then following directions that vary from product to product. We have included a lovely "dill pickle" sauerkraut that kids who enjoy more sour flavors *love*. Due to the probiotics in these dishes, your kids can benefit from better digestion and increased immune function. Studies show that kids who enjoy healthy probiotics daily are more protected from catching common cold and flu strains. These recipes are most easily enjoyed as a topping for various dishes throughout the book or can be used in fillings for wraps, sandwiches, and hand-helds. The Chia Coconut Fermented Yogurt (page 208) can be an add-in to breakfasts and desserts as well.

Donna Gates, author of *The Body Ecology Diet*, shares that "kids do very well" on a diet that includes probiotic-rich fermented foods. Her book and program outline the root cause of many food allergies and issues in adrenal function: an unhealthy gut. At a time when more and more kids are born with these issues, science is taking a closer look at the reasons why. We find here that health is passed down generationally, and through the field of epigenetics, we are beginning to see the links between a number of current-day health concerns, especially in children, and the poor diet of the family line long before conception.

Mind-blowing? Well, yes. Prior to this, the idea was that our body was really our own personal domain, and the thinking was "to each his own" with respect to food choices. Current studies are dispelling that myth, however, and although we cannot reverse the clock or the damage, we have an opportunity for understanding the "why" behind some of our current pediatric health concerns that have been handed down through the past two generations. This is an empowering understanding for parents, strengthening their resolve to make healthy foods available for the family. It also reminds us to teach our kids as we go so that *they* understand the "why" behind the food choices the family is making.

In this case, fermented foods are a great tool to help restore the balance in the gut and create some new digestive health opportunities for our children. Having a strong digestive function, coupled with a powerful immune system, is a result of daily food choices, and fermented foods are a simple option you can "add in" to a traditional meal.

CHIA COCONUT FERMENTED YOGURT

Coconut yogurt is the perfect base recipe for creating breakfast parfaits, topping desserts, and enjoying fresh with a slice of seasonal fruit. You can make this recipe once per week and allow it to ferment throughout the week for additional healthy probiotics.

INGREDIENTS	INSTRUCTIONS
2 cups coconut flesh	In a blender, combine all the ingredients and blend on high speed until a rich and thick crème has formed.
½ cup coconut water	
2 tablespoons lemon juice	Transfer the mixture to a glass container. Refrigerate until ready to use.
2 tablespoons raw sweetener of choice	
2 tablespoons white chia seeds	*For probiotics, basic acidophilus can be used or other varieties, such as Friendly Force by Healthforce Nutritionals. Even a liquid fermented coconut kefir like inner-ēco is an easy option that can be used simply to get the probiotic benefit right away. Pay attention to your body's reactions to fermented foods, as some people have histamine sensitivities that can result in itching and other skin conditions, bloating, and racing heart. Discontinuing the food usually stops these symptoms, but do check with your physician if symptoms continue.
2 servings powdered probiotics*	

Makes 16 ounces

RAW

DILL PICKLE SAUERKRAUT

❧

Sauerkraut is a nice condiment to have available to spice up any salad or entrée. It's a basic that kids who enjoy sour flavors typically take to. This sauerkraut will also last for 2 to 3 weeks in the refrigerator.

INGREDIENTS	INSTRUCTIONS
4 cups shredded cabbage	In a large mixing bowl, massage the cabbage with the sea salt.
1 teaspoon sea salt	
1 cup diced or sliced dill pickles	Add in the pickles, seeds, and water, and transfer the entire mixture to a 24-ounce mason jar.
2 tablespoons caraway seeds	
½ cup water	Pack the mixture down into the mason jar. Let sit on the counter out of direct sunlight for up to 3 days. Press the mixture down every 4 to 8 hours for the first 24 hours for best results.
	Once the fermentation process begins, at day 3, refrigerate and use within the upcoming month.

Makes 2 cups

RAW

ALMOND CRÈME

This is a nice, soft, ripe cheese, essentially, and can be used for up to a month at a time. It is best placed in a 12-ounce ramekin for easy scooping and spreading, because it becomes thicker as it sits.

INGREDIENTS	INSTRUCTIONS
1 cup raw almonds ½ cup almond mylk ¼ cup lemon juice 2 tablespoons acidophilus 1 tablespoon raw sweetener of choice 1 teaspoon sea salt	In a blender, blend all the ingredients until well combined. Transfer the mixture to a ramekin and cover with cheesecloth or plastic wrap. If covering with wrap, poke a few holes in the top to allow airflow over the top of the mixture. Leave out for 2 to 3 days until the mixture begins to ripen. Then transfer to the refrigerator and enjoy throughout the entire month. This mixture is nice on a cheese platter or in place of spreadable cheeses like cream cheese. The important thing to remember is that the mixture will continue to ripen throughout the month, even in the refrigerator, so the flavor and consistency will continue to evolve. Many Veggie Mamas report that they enjoy this crème the most about 7 days after preparation!

Makes 12 ounces

RAW

SPROUTED, FERMENTED SESAME MYLK

Veggie kids who have challenges with allergies find this mylk a welcome relief. Simple to prepare, it's made from soaked and sprouted sesame seeds. Sesame seeds are naturally high in calcium and iron, so this mylk is also a great option for building healthy brains and bodies. You may wish to add 2 tablespoons chia seeds to the blender for additional omega fatty acids or 2 tablespoons hemp seeds for additional protein.

INGREDIENTS	INSTRUCTIONS
1 cup soaked sesame seeds	Blend all the ingredients in a basic blender on high speed until well combined.
1½ cups water	
1 tablespoon acidophilus or other powdered probiotic	Transfer the mylk to a storage container that can easily be refrigerated. We love mason jars for this use in particular.
1 tablespoon raw coconut nectar or raw honey	This mylk will be good for 7 to 14 days.
1 pinch sea salt	Shake the blend prior to use so the natural sediment is combined for best enjoyment.

Makes 16 ounces

RAW

FERMENTED-VEGETABLE ARAME MIX

—✦—

This recipe combines naturally salty sea vegetables—a fun and easy way to get in additional minerals to support optimal health—with grounding root vegetables and miso paste. Fermented miso paste has been shown to help protect the body against radiation and can also help make the potassium in this side-dish mix more bioavailable.

INGREDIENTS	INSTRUCTIONS
1 tablespoon white miso paste	In a small bowl, whisk together the miso paste, coconut aminos, ginger juice, and sweetener of choice.
2 tablespoons coconut aminos	
1 tablespoon ginger juice (optional)	In a medium mixing bowl, toss together the arame, carrots, beets, sesame seeds, and cashews until well combined.
1 teaspoon raw honey or raw coconut nectar	
1 cup soaked arame	Add the miso mixture to the vegetables and toss together until all the vegetables are well coated.
½ cup shredded carrots	
½ cup shredded purple beets	Let sit for 20 minutes before serving so the flavors can blend. Refrigerate all leftovers for up to 7 days.
2 tablespoons black sesame seeds	
⅓ cup raw cashews or raw pumpkin seeds	

Makes 16 ounces

RAW

Chapter 11

VEGGIE MAMA KID-PARTY PLATTERS AND PLANT-POWERED ENTERTAINING

For toddlers through elementary-school-age kids, parties are the thing. Children's parties can be a fabulous way for a prepared Veggie Mama to show off her favorite family recipes—and provide a little neighborly health inspiration at the same time. Celebration can be a challenge when you are first transitioning your dietary lifestyle and the shift is still under way. However, as you become more confident in the kitchen and your family's health improves, you will have much to celebrate!

This chapter provides some tips for success and some ideas for menus and snacks to make sure your offerings are healthy, fun, and fresh. Children's parties are all about the look of the table spread, since we eat with our eyes first at every age, so this is a great time to get creative and "play" with your food! As we have illustrated in the book up to this point, healthy options can truly be simple and fun. And as we move toward the conclusion, you will find many of these celebratory ideas may become weekly staples in your very own Veggie Mama kitchen!

The following recipes can be incorporated into get-togethers of all sizes and themes. Most kids in this age category are only going to graze at events because there is so much to do with friends and family! So these snacks can double as entrée options or as a key part of a buffet. We have included recipes with different serving sizes that can be easily multiplied for larger groups as well.

Veggie Mama Idea for the Adventurous Family:
Party-Food Favors

Lots of moms want to send their guests home with simple and affordable gifts! Here are some activities and easy grab-bag favors that kids can make and take or your family can prepare in advance. This is a great way to share your food lifestyle and also inspire other families in your community.

FAVORS TO TAKE AND MAKE

Bugs on a Log: All you need is sunflower seed butter, raisins, and celery sticks for an interactive activity that can be then packed in rolled-up paper bags or food trays and wrapped in cellophane.

Berry Baskets: If you are enjoying a party around berry season, you can purchase mini berry baskets and provide decorations that can be glued to them. Then invite the kids to fill with fresh berries from a bowl in the center of the table.

Raw-Foods Candy Boxes: The dough from the Cashew Chocolate Sweets recipe (page 177) can be hand rolled by the kids as an activity. Then purchase candy boxes for them to fill and then decorate on the outside as a nice treat to go!

FAVORS TO MAKE AND PACKAGE IN ADVANCE

Trail-Mix Cones: Fill some cone-shaped cellophane bags with Nut-Free Trail Mix (page 192). This favor can double as an extra snack for hungry kiddos and is especially good for parties at the park!

Dried Fruits: If you have a dehydrator or low-temperature oven, you can dehydrate a variety of fruits and then package them in clear cellophane bags with fancy ribbons for a nice treat.

Cookies and Tea: Make some Easy Cookies (page 181) and then place them in paper bags and wrap them up with your favorite loose-leaf teas! You can even find teacups at the local thrift shop to put them in as a fun presentation.

FAVORS THAT GROW

Pots with Seeds: Small pots and packages of seeds can be an easy spring favor for both girls' and boys' parties.

Wheatgrass Patches: Wheatgrass is easy to cut into small squares, which then can be set at each child's place with decorations like small pinwheels sticking out.

Herb Sprouts: As an activity, you can provide halved orange or other citrus peels that kids can plant with herb sprouts! This doubles as a party favor as well!

WATERMELON PIZZA SLICES

·❧·

This recipe is a fun and flavorful take on a "veggie pizza," plus it's visually interesting and creative to boot. These slices can be prepared up to 2 hours in advance and kept chilled in the refrigerator. You can also make "whole" pizzas by cutting large rounds of watermelon instead of wedge slices.

INGREDIENTS	INSTRUCTIONS
For the pizza:	For the pizza, set up the watermelon round on the cutting board.
1 large round of watermelon, 1 inch thick	Evenly layer it with all the topping ingredients.
1 cup diced tomatoes	For the sauce, if you would like to offer an additional sauce option, blend all the sauce ingredients in the blender on high speed until rich and creamy. Top the pizza with dollops of "sauce."
1 cup shredded carrots	
1 cup cauliflower "cheese"*	
1 cup diced pineapple	
½ cup Daiya mozzarella cheese (optional)	*For the "cheese," cut the very tops off cauliflower florets to mimic a Parmesan-cheese look.
For the sauce (optional):	
1 cup walnut pieces	
½ cup water	
¼ cup raw sweetener of choice	
1 clove garlic	
1 pinch sea salt	

Makes 4 servings

RAW

THE "SMOOTHIE" BAR

Kids love fruit! And fruit smoothie bars are a great way to share a healthy life-style and also be allergy conscious when entertaining larger groups. It's helpful to have a base smoothie blend to which you can add special superfoods and unique fruits. Mason jars are easy to dress up and look nice on a buffet as well, especially when you tie on special ribbons or twine to decorate your gathering. You can also add special tags with each guest's name. Paper straws with stripes or thick straws are a fun way to further enhance the look of the smoothie bar!

INGREDIENTS

For the smoothie base:

6 bananas

1 cup apple juice

For the add-ins:

2 cups chopped mango

2 cups chopped pineapple

2 cups sliced strawberries

1 cup coconut shreds

1 cup diced avocado

Ice

For the garnish to the jar or glass:

½ cup coconut shreds

INSTRUCTIONS

For the smoothie base, in a blender, combine the bananas and apple juice and blend on high speed until a liquid is formed. Transfer to a glass pitcher for easy pouring.

For the add-ins, set up a blender where guests have easy access to it. Invite them to combine ½ cup base and ½ cup add-ins, along with a scoop of ice, and blend up their own concoction!

For the garnish, place the coconut pieces next to a small bowl of water. Show guests how to dip the rim of their jar into the water and then into the coco-nut for a fancy way to garnish the glass.

In addition, we recommend garnishing each smoothie with more fresh fruits before serving.

Makes eight 8—ounce servings | RAW

FROZEN FRUIT GELATO

—✦—

This is as basic as it gets when it comes to easy-to-execute recipes. You can purchase frozen organic fruits or freeze your own leftovers throughout the year to use in this simple dish. Be sure to add loads of fun toppings as well: chopped nuts, fresh fruits, and dried coconut and berries are delicious, healthier toppings. This mix can even be scooped out and served on gluten-free ice-cream cones!

INGREDIENTS	INSTRUCTIONS
4 cups frozen fruits	In a blender, blend all the ingredients on high speed until a rich, frozen crème is formed.
1 cup frozen banana	
½ cup water*	
2 tablespoons raw sweetener of choice	Divide the mixture equally among 4 serving bowls. Garnish with the toppings of your choice and enjoy!
1 pinch sea salt	
	*For a richer variation, substitute almond mylk for the water.

ZUCCHINI PIZZA STICKS

This is a variation on the recipe earlier in the book for the Marinara Zucchini Sticks (page 159). For this party presentation, we warm the sticks in the dehydrator and serve with added toppings that each child chooses.

Pull out mini "pizza" pans and place the already-cooked zucchini sticks on them for each portion. (You can find these pans, which make a fun themed presentation for the zucchini sticks, at kitchen-supply stores.) Then as guests arrive, offer the following toppings:

INGREDIENTS	INSTRUCTIONS
Vegan cheese Almond meal Fresh herbs, like basil and oregano Cheesy Cauliflower (page 156) Nutritional yeast	Help each guest layer the pan with desired toppings and dehydrate in the dehydrator set on high for 30 minutes while engaged in other activities. If you don't yet have a dehydrator, you can warm these in an oven set at 250°F for 3 to 5 minutes.

Servings: Varied

ZOODLES OF FUN!

Zoodles, or "zucchini noodles," take on the flavor of whatever sauce they are prepared with. A variation on the simple everyday version in your weekly meal-planning guide, this recipe is made with a "spiralizing" tool or can be duplicated on a mandoline using the julienne blade. If you have a spiralizing tool, this activity is great fun to encourage participation in your celebration. We have also included three variations here for your zoodle parties so that you can give them a fusion flair! Be sure to keep things interesting by adding as many toppings as you'd like!

INGREDIENTS	INSTRUCTIONS
6 zucchini	Work with guests to create zoodles from the zucchini using a spiralizing machine.
For the varieties:	Add the desired toppings to the bowl and pass around for all participants to contribute to the tossing.
## ITALIAN	Top with the desired sauces.
2 cups diced Roma tomatoes	Serve in a noodle bowl with chopsticks for a fun, festive option, or place in Chinese take-out boxes on a buffet.
1 cup olives	
2 cups Sweet Pesto (page 53)	
## ASIAN	
2 cups shredded carrots or carrot curls	
1 cup chopped cashews or walnuts	
2 tablespoons sesame seeds	
1 cup Sweet Ginger Sauce (page 142)	
## AMERICAN	
2 cups Cheesy Cauliflower (orange cauliflower, if possible) (page 156)	
1 cup diced avocado	
2 tablespoons nutritional yeast	
1 cup Alfredo Sauce (page 143)	

Makes 6 servings | RAW

FRUIT AND VEGETABLE SKEWERS & SNACK SHAPES

Melons are easy to form into multiple shapes using cookie cutters. They can then be arranged on a platter or slid onto a skewer. Here are a few Veggie Mama favorites to help you highlight the fruit tray at your next gathering.

INGREDIENTS	INSTRUCTIONS
1 small watermelon (will only be using half)	Begin by cutting the watermelon in half. Place the cut side facedown on the cutting board and cut slices 1½ inches thick. Transfer to a large cutting board, placing slices flat now. Using a heart- or star-shaped cookie cutter about 3 inches in overall diameter, cut out melon shapes. Place the shapes in a bowl.
4 kiwis	
3 cups grapes	
2 cups large strawberries	
	Remove the skins of the kiwi, cut into round segments ¾ inch thick, and place in a small bowl.
	Rinse the grapes well and chill in another small bowl before using.
	Cut the strawberries in half from top to bottom so they resemble hearts and place in a small bowl.
	You may wish to offer an activity where guests make their own skewers. If so, lay out a large platter to collect the skewers and then assemble the bowls of prepared fruit all around it. Provide bamboo skewers that are 6 inches long for best results.
	If you will be arranging the fruit, alternate colors and shapes on the skewers for a festive fruit tray, or if you are short on time, simply assemble in rows on a platter for guests to enjoy.

Makes 6 servings | RAW

COOKIE BARS

Cookie bars are easy to create with a great raw dough. This is an enjoyable group activity, and guests can make their own party favors if you offer small canning jars or origami papers to wrap their cookies. For best results, make 3 batches of the Simple Crust for a party of 10; this way, everyone can make 2 to 4 treats.

INGREDIENTS	INSTRUCTIONS
Simple Crust (page 180) Raw Cookie Dough (page 170) Toppings of your choice	Set up 3 separate stations (put small plates on each so guests can easily move around with their cookies): *Station 1:* Place a roller and a covered cutting board, along with a variety of cookie cutters. *Station 2:* Place a variety of toppings for kids to roll ball shapes in, as well as an ice-cream scoop so they can scoop out round sections of dough. *Station 3:* Place craft supplies like confection paper, craft paper, and candy boxes with various stickers so they can easily wrap up their treats to take them home!

Servings: Varied

RAW

GORILLA BOWLS

Gorillas are the strongest animals in the jungle, and they are vegan, too! For zoo-themed parties or an all-out monkeying-around good time, these bowls are a sweet treat that also contain some important nutrients—*shhh* . . . that's our little secret!

INGREDIENTS

For the bowl base:

4 cups diced jicama

1 cup Cheesy Cauliflower Sauce (page 156)

For the bowl topping:

2 cups diced banana (cut these into odd-shaped sizes for the best crowd reactions)

1 cup diced kiwi

1 cup red or green grapes, cut in half

1 cup granola of choice (or recipe on page 64)

1 cup nuts or seeds of choice

¼ cup coconut flakes

INSTRUCTIONS

For the bowl base, in a medium mixing bowl, toss the jicama in the sauce and let sit while preparing the topping.

For the bowl topping, in a separate medium bowl, combine the banana, kiwi, grapes, granola, and nuts. Toss these together well, but gently, so the banana stays nice and firm.

Divide the base among 6 bowls or themed jungle plates.

Garnish with the topping mix and then sprinkle with the coconut flakes.

This is best served at room temperature or chilled.

Makes 6 servings

RAW

STUFFED ORANGES

Simple citrus can really steal the show if you top it right. I (Jenny) love combining oranges with avocado and coconut in order to provide healthy fats in an easy treat form.

INGREDIENTS	INSTRUCTIONS
4 oranges	Cut the oranges in half, and then cut out the insides using a serrated knife; transfer to a cutting board. Set these orange "cups" aside. Dice the orange insides into ½-inch pieces.
1 Hass avocado, peeled, pitted, and diced	
¼ cup coconut flakes	
1 pinch sea salt	In a medium bowl, combine the chopped orange, avocado, coconut, and salt. Toss well.
	To prepare the stuffed oranges, fill in the orange cups with the avocado-coconut filling.

Makes 4 servings | RAW

ARTICHOKE AND SPINACH DIP

Artichokes are high in potassium and phytonutrients, supporting the immune system and also the bones and connective tissues by providing a valuable mineral. At the same time, artichoke hearts are a good source of dietary fiber. As a result, when you enjoy them, you will feel full and satiated with less food *and* they will benefit your body. Pairing the artichokes with spinach—supplying protein and minerals—gives you even more nutrition.

For those who enjoy dips with texture, this one is nice and thick and can easily be dipped into with celery or carrot sticks or South of the Border Baked Crisps (page 150). You may wish to offer a bulk serving in the middle of the table surrounded by all three dipping options. Any transitional crudité platter options will taste great with this dip as well.

INGREDIENTS

16 ounces artichoke hearts, canned or frozen

2 cups baby spinach

1 tablespoon extra-virgin olive oil

3 tablespoons Veganaise (plant- and oil-based creamy spread) or Tahini Sauce (page 141)

1 tablespoon chile-garlic salt

⅓ cup nondairy cheese alternative (optional)

INSTRUCTIONS

Preheat the oven to 350°F.

In a food processor with the S-blade attachment in place or using a blender, pulse the artichoke hearts to a chunky consistency. Remove the hearts and set aside. Then, using the same food processor with the S-blade attachment still in place or the blender, pulse the

INSTRUCTIONS, CONT'D.

spinach and olive oil until well chopped, being careful not to overprocess to a creamy consistency. Set aside the spinach mixture.

In a medium mixing bowl, toss together the artichoke chunks, spinach mixture, Veganaise, and chile-garlic salt. Mix with a spatula until well combined. Place the dip mixture in a glass baking dish and sprinkle with the cheese alternative, if desired.

Bake for 15 minutes. The mixture should be golden brown on the top. Serve immediately with South of the Border Baked Crisps or other vegetable crudités. This dip may also be saved in the refrigerator for up to 3 days in an airtight container. Turn this dish into a meal by adding it alongside a fresh vegetable soup or entrée salad!

Makes 4 snack-size servings

BANANA SUSHI ROLLS

This is a fun and simple presentation and also makes a great activity at a party. Using easy-to-find nori wraps and nut or seed butter, you can duplicate "sushi" rolls with bananas!

INGREDIENTS

6 bananas

6 nori sheets

12 tablespoons raw nut or seed butter

For optional garnishes:

1 cup coconut shreds

¼ cup hemp seeds

1 cup dried rice cereal (rice only, no sweetener)

INSTRUCTIONS

Remove the banana skins and discard.

With the matte side up, roll the nori sheet tightly around the banana. Then use a knife to coat each nori roll in 2 tablespoons nut butter.

Roll the sticky rolls in the garnish of choice and slice into bite-size pieces!

Makes 6 'sushi' rolls   RAW

AFTERWORD

We hope that after taking in the information and the recipes in this book, you find yourself inspired and empowered to create a food culture in your own home that fosters wellness of body and mind. Our children are entrusted to us for a short time so that we may provide tools and resources for them to grow and become the light of the world. Food plays an integral role in this parenting commitment.

This book was born of our impulse to share the simple steps and tools that can make clean plant-based foods a foundation for the optimal health of your family. Our planet is constantly changing, and so are our food options. However, as we've outlined in this book, the food options that offer the highest level of nutrition are as old as life on earth. They are inherited gifts from Mother Nature. Food grown *on* a plant, not manufactured *in* a plant, can deeply nourish your children and carry them into their own passion and purpose in life in a powerful way.

There is no greater gift a parent can endow their loved ones with than a lifestyle full of healthy habits that they can take forward into their own families and pass down. If we focus on creating a lifestyle centered around nourishing whole foods, we can help heal some of the broken links in wellness at our current time in history, leaving future generations tools for a more vibrant world.

Once you understand the truth of health, your spark has been ignited and you cannot go back. We encourage you to share what resonates with you from this book with your friends and your community—to become a confident and outspoken Veggie Mama who says, "It worked for me; it can work for you too!"

May you and your family enjoy vibrant health in every way!

— Doreen and Jenny

APPENDIX

Vegan Preconception and Pregnancy Planning

From the moment you decide to bring life into the world, you have already begun the process of breaking down your own mental barriers about your personal limitations and the sacrifices you are willing to make. You are consciously summoning powerful untapped energies that can help you evolve your pregnancy and create a healthy lifestyle for growing healthy kids.

From preconception to birth, your body will be changing so quickly that it may seem difficult to keep up with all the milestones! The good news is, as you advance in your pregnancy, your needs from start to finish really are the same: good clean water, and lots of it; high-protein, vitamin- and mineral-dense foods for growing healthy skeletal structure; and healthy fats for developing brain tissue. All of this will need to be balanced with healthy whole carbs to create energy enough for two beings.

Hearing that may seem overwhelming at first, but we are going to guide you with some simple and natural ideas to create a food plan for pregnancy that will keep you feeling invigorated and well throughout.

During pregnancy, aligning your nutritional needs will be an exercise in planning and balance. You will need to plan your food for the week if "eating clean" is a priority. You will also need to be sure you consume enough calories and that those calories are well balanced so that nothing is lacking. This dance of planning and balance is a skill set that you will call upon once your child arrives, so getting used to these steps at this stage can set you up for future success with your family.

The important thing here is to begin with the end in mind. If you require 2,000 to 2,600 calories, depending on your stage of pregnancy, from five fresh meals a day, you will need to start out by shopping for some fresh produce and some pantry ingredients that will fuel your week.

To supplement the information in Chapter 3, we have included a shopping list here that you can adapt to create healthy meals that nurture your pregnancy. This list is divided by nutrients. For example, you will see notes for shopping for plant-based proteins, essential fatty acids or "healthy fats," and whole-food carbohydrates. You will

have 60 percent higher blood volume during pregnancy, so minerals like iron and calcium will be important, and those resources are on the list too (see page 240)!

From this shopping list, we have created virtually all the recipes in this book, so you can imagine that our pantry looks the same as yours will as you adopt some of the rituals and processes contained in these pages.

PLANT-BASED PROTEINS		
SOURCE	GRAMS OF PROTEIN PER SERVING	SERVING SIZE
Lentils	17.9	1 cup (raw)
Split peas	48.4	1 cup (raw)
Buckwheat	22.5	1 cup (raw)
Quinoa	24	1 cup (raw)
Dark leafy greens	5	2 cups (raw)
Avocado	4	1¼ cups (raw)
Pumpkin seeds	33.9	1 cup (raw)
Sunflower seeds	9.6	1 cup (raw)
Hemp seeds	12	2 tablespoons (raw)
Garbanzo beans	38.6	1 cup (raw)
Spirulina	1.7*	1 ounce

*This amount of protein may seem low, but spirulina is made up of 60% protein by volume, in addition to chlorophyll and important minerals.

FRESH FRUITS AND VEGETABLES

Apples

Basil

Blueberries

Broccoli

Carrots

Cherries

Cilantro

Cucumbers

Green onions

Kale

Mangos

Mint

Peaches

Pears

Pineapple

Red bell peppers

Red chard

Spinach

Strawberries

Zucchini

WHOLE-FOOD CARBOHYDRATES

Black beans

Brown rice

Buckwheat

Butternut squash

Quinoa

Sweet potatoes

Yams

Zucchini

HEALTHY FATS

Almond butter

Almonds

Avocado

Coconut

Olives

Pecans

Pumpkin seeds

Sesame seeds

Sunflower seeds

Walnuts

SUPERFOODS

Chia seeds

Gogi berries

Hemp seeds

Raw cacao

Spirulina

Veggie Mama Healthy Habits

Once you have shopped the stores in your area for the best ingredients, you are now ready to begin with three healthy habits for every Veggie Mama adopting a vegan pregnancy.

Veggie Mama Healthy Habit #1: Five a Day

Eat five main meals a day! Your blood sugar will be the most balanced, and your body will stay best alkalized, if you eat five smaller meals a day throughout your pregnancy. We know that staying alkalized helps stave off nausea from morning sickness, so this will be an important key to feeling great during your pregnancy. Alkalizing your body will also reduce inflammation to keep you moving well even into your third trimester, where it is common for pregnant women to begin to experience some discomfort from swelling in the joints, especially the ankles. For more alkalizing foods, refer to our reference chart (pages 20–21)

as a go-to guide for quick options to alkalize your body during pregnancy and beyond.

Veggie Mama Healthy Habit #2: Maintain Balance

Eat balanced meals at every mealtime. It's important to take a look at your "pregnancy" plate from a plant-powered perspective. You'll want to be sure you have more than 50 percent of the plate filled with fresh whole fruits and vegetables of different colors and textures. The color of each fruit and vegetable represents different minerals and vitamins. A colorful array ensures a variety of essential nutrients. The texture represents different moisture contents. You'll need to source an extra 20 percent or more of healthy hydration during your pregnancy. The remaining 50 percent of your plate should be composed of plant-based proteins and healthy fats. The important thing to remember when setting up your meal plan is that your body will be using the protein and fat to feed your brain—and your baby's—and then to support your vital organs.

½ FRESH FRUITS & VEGETABLES

includes your carbs, vitamins, and minerals (such as 1 cup broccoli, 2 cups salad of dark leafy greens, 2 cups veggie mix)

¼ PROTEIN

(such as 1 cup beans, 1½ cups quinoa, 3 tablespoons hemp seeds)

¼ HEALTHY ESSENTIAL FATS

(such as ½ avocado, 2 tablespoons almond butter, ½ cup nuts or seeds)

Also check your plate to see what micro-nutrients are represented. In particular, ask yourself where is the **iron, calcium, folate,** and **vitamin** C in my meal? You can always add a quick garnish of beans, fruits, or seeds to balance the nutrition of your plate!

HIGH-IRON FOODS

Almonds

Black beans

Buckwheat

Dark leafy greens

Garbanzo beans

Quinoa

Sesame seeds

Sunflower seeds

Tahini

Walnuts

HIGH-FOLATE FOODS

Black beans

Broccoli

Dark leafy greens

Garbanzo beans

Kidney beans

Lentils

HIGH-CALCIUM FOODS

Broccoli

Dark leafy greens

Dried apricots

Figs

Kiwis

Oranges

HIGH–VITAMIN C FOODS

Cherries

Gogi berries

Kiwis

Oranges

Red bell peppers

Strawberries

Pregnancy Nutrition Reminders

— **Calories.** A healthy consumption of calories each day can help you maintain energy and balance. The American Pregnancy Association recommends an extra 300 calories per trimester as you advance through your pregnancy.

— **Hydration.** You need 20 to 30 percent more water intake during pregnancy. Meal plans high in living raw foods will help achieve this due to their natural moisture content. Our meals are designed with this important need in mind.

— **Important minerals.** Be sure to enjoy foods with the following key minerals in abundance. The daily requirements are listed here for pregnant and nursing women; however, mineral-rich foods cannot be overdone during this important time. Your body feeds your baby first by design; you get the leftovers for your own vital functions. With this in mind, be sure you get in healthy amounts of:

- Folate: 400 mcg daily, found in dark leafy greens, lentils, beans, and broccoli

- Iron: 18 or more mg per day, found in tahini, sunflower seeds, nuts, dark leafy greens, whole grains, and beans

- Calcium: 1,200 mg per day, found in leafy greens, beans, fruits, and broccoli

- Vitamin C: 85 mg, found in citrus, goji berries, cherries, strawberries, kiwis, and red bell peppers

- Magnesium: 350 mg, found in almonds, spinach, black beans, cashews, and avocado

Veggie Mama Healthy Habit #3: Plan Ahead

Pregnancy can bring on a wide array of shifts in hormone and energy levels—and, as a result, your mood! Planning ahead is an important part of maintaining a balanced and healthy meal program when expecting. Additionally, this step can support your overall wellness by forming a habit that allows your body to fall into a routine, ensuring important nutritional cornerstones are met throughout the day. Distractions abound in the modern world we live in, and we are more motivated when we have a healthy pattern to look forward to. Studies show that building in routines makes us more effective in achieving our goals. If *your* goal is a healthy and vibrant pregnancy, following the advice in this book to preplan your meals for the week can help you reach it and exceed your expectations!

♥

VEGAN POSTPARTUM

One great benefit of enjoying a plant-strong pregnancy is that your body is supported, making your transition time as a new mom more enjoyable and balanced. During postpartum, your body will be moving through a significant hormonal shift and readjustment. If you're strong and well nourished going in, this transition can be more peaceful. It's of utmost importance that you continue with the Veggie Mama healthy habits to maintain as much balance as possible as you advance out of your pregnancy and into postpartum. Your decision to do so can mean the difference between enjoying these in-between moments and feeling out of control during this time. Every pregnancy is different and every birth its own divine miracle, but food supports the universal importance of a healthy, well-balanced diet during a positive transition into motherhood.

Here are some key areas of nutrition to focus on from post-pregnancy through lactation:

Important Minerals

Calcium

1,000 mg calcium is the daily requirement for lactating mothers. Achieving this on a plant-based diet is relatively easy as long as you eat or drink your greens, as a salad or morning smoothie—for example, the Mama's Morning Smoothie (page 82) or the Sweet Kale Salad (page 134). You can enjoy 4 cups fresh dark leafy greens to satisfy the full requirement, or have a combination of other favorites like almonds or almond butter (94 to 111 mg per 2 tablespoons), tahini (128 mg per 2 tablespoons), and beans (126 mg per cup cooked, or ½ cup sprouted). See the shopping list for other ideas for high-calcium foods to add to your menus.

Iron

50 mg iron is the daily requirement for postpartum women. Pumpkin seeds (1 ounce) and quinoa (4 ounces) contain more than 4 mg per serving and also double as proteins, so these are great options. Sea vegetables are easy to add to just about everything, making them a ready source of iron. We recommend dulse flakes as salty-tasting additions to hummus, guacamole, and salads. If you don't feel you are able to consume enough iron, it is important to find a clean supplement to make sure you are supporting adequate blood production and healthy nursing and milk production. Note that caffeine and alcohol consumption block the absorption of iron, so consider abstaining from these substances during this time of new motherhood.

Healthy Fats

In postpartum, your brain can play tricks on you, altering your mood as your hormone levels shift. While nursing, you will notice a surge in serotonin and the "love" hormone oxytocin as a nice benefit to breast-feeding. However, in between it is common to feel lethargic, moody, or emotional. To help stay balanced throughout the day, healthy fats like avocado, coconut, coconut oil as a supplement, pumpkin seeds, and the superfoods chia and hemp seeds are great choices to support your overall feelings of happiness as a new Veggie Mama.

Nutrient-Dense Foods

I (Jenny) noticed that when I was first nursing and pumping while away from my babies, I ate so many greens that my breast milk was literally tinted green! This was a powerful example of how your body converts nutrients for your baby's developmental needs. Breast-feeding plays a documented role in forging a bond between babies and their mothers and also in healthy brain development. The nutrient density of your food is of key importance in order for all of those benefits to line up for the highest good of all.

Living plant-based foods that have not been cooked above 118°F preserve the maximum number of nutrients in every bite, as well as offer essential enzymes needed as a catalyst for the body to properly absorb the nutrients. The focus of this plan will be to include a significant amount of living plant-based foods for this very reason. From prepregnancy on, you will notice the benefits of increased energy, incredible vitality, and also healthy regularity of the digestive tract.

Fiber

Fiber plays a critical role in assisting the work of the digestive tract. Plant-based fibers are the best for maintaining this regularity. This is why juicing is not recommended during pregnancy through the postpartum nursing period. You can use juice as a vitamin/mineral supplement, as in the case of a low-sugar green juice, but it should not replace a meal. Overall, smoothies with the fibers blended in can be considered a healthy meal, and whole foods are the best choice for maintaining adequate fiber and thereby easy digestion. The reality is that many women complain of constipation during and after pregnancy. However, if your nutrition is on point, integrating plant-strong fibers, this should not be an issue.

Superfoods

Superfoods can play an especially important nutritional role in pregnancy and postpartum, because you get a concentrated amount of key nutrients in a small package. Simple to integrate into meals, they can help you boost intake of protein and minerals without having to invest significant time in the kitchen. When 2 tablespoons hemp seeds provide 14 grams of protein, it's easy to add this ingredient to a smoothie or sprinkle onto a salad and get on with your day. Superfoods are not *supplements* in the traditional definition of the word because they are not isolates, but rather whole foods with big "super" benefits. They can be used to "supplement" your whole plant-based diet with key nutrients, which is why this terminology can seem confusing.

Nursing

When nursing, you up your daily energy intake another 300 calories above your body's needs when pregnant. So, yes, it's good to eat even more once you begin nursing. This will naturally taper off over time, but in the first six to nine months, your baby will need that rich, nourishing milk to form positive synapses in the brain, grow strong bones, and further develop internal organs. During this time, it's beneficial to drink your extra calories. I (Jenny) created the following beverage when nursing to keep me going between meals, especially in the morning when my kids would nurse the most.

MAMA'S MYLK

1 cup almond mylk or other nut or seed mylk

2 tablespoons hemp seeds

1 tablespoon greens (spirulina, Dr. Schulze supergreens, or chlorella)

1 tablespoon coconut butter or oil

Vanilla paste, to taste

Ground cinnamon, to taste

Some other ideas for getting in more beneficial calories include the Chocolate Chia Pudding (page 167), the Coconut Crème Soup (page 131), and the Deviled Tomatoes (page 153). All three options are high in fat content and are satisfying for nursing moms. One fellow nursing mom remarked to me, "I just can't stop thinking about food," and then asked me what I do. I shared that the more filling the calories, the less I focused on food. Many calories are "empty," and when you're pregnant and nursing, it's a natural time to avoid foods that don't pack a nutritional punch. While quick snack foods may seem abundant in today's world, these foods are no friend to you in your time of need and in fact will have to be balanced by other rich sources of nourishment later.

It's a fact that when you eat fried foods, for example, an acidic reaction is triggered in the body, throwing off the natural pH balance, creating inflammation and blocking nutrient absorption. This is something that healthy mamas need to avoid if they want to experience strong, happy pregnancies and nursing moments.

The water content of your food is another important point of focus for nursing mothers, just like during pregnancy. Our bodies are more than 75 percent water, and a nursing mom will be the first to tell you how much extra water is necessary to feel hydrated. Technically speaking, you need 3 to 4 cups more water per day when nursing. So besides additional intake of healthy fluids, like water and raw coconut water, it is imperative that your food be a rich source of hydration. In this case, be sure to enjoy at least 80 percent fresh living foods on every plate, like in our Veggie Mama design! This choice will provide hydrating benefits for your nursing body.

METRIC CONVERSION CHART

The recipes in this book use the standard United States method for measuring liquid and dry or solid ingredients (teaspoons, tablespoons, and cups). The following charts are provided to help cooks outside the U.S. successfully use these recipes. All equivalents are approximate.

Standard Cup	Fine Powder (e.g., flour)	Grain (e.g., rice)	Granular (e.g., sugar)	Liquid Solids (e.g., butter)	Liquid (e.g., milk)
1	140 g	150 g	190 g	200 g	240 ml
¾	105 g	113 g	143 g	150 g	180 ml
⅔	93 g	100 g	125 g	133 g	160 ml
½	70 g	75 g	95 g	100 g	120 ml
⅓	47 g	50 g	63 g	67 g	80 ml
¼	35 g	38 g	48 g	50 g	60 ml
⅛	18 g	19 g	24 g	25 g	30 ml

Useful Equivalents for Liquid Ingredients by Volume				
¼ tsp				1 ml
½ tsp				2 ml
1 tsp				5 ml
3 tsp	1 tbsp		½ fl oz	15 ml
	2 tbsp	⅛ cup	1 fl oz	30 ml
	4 tbsp	¼ cup	2 fl oz	60 ml
	5⅓ tbsp	⅓ cup	3 fl oz	80 ml
	8 tbsp	½ cup	4 fl oz	120 ml
	10⅔ tbsp	⅔ cup	5 fl oz	160 ml
	12 tbsp	¾ cup	6 fl oz	180 ml
	16 tbsp	1 cup	8 fl oz	240 ml
	1 pt	2 cups	16 fl oz	480 ml
	1 qt	4 cups	32 fl oz	960 ml
			33 fl oz	1000 ml	1 l

Useful Equivalents for Dry Ingredients by Weight

(To convert ounces to grams, multiply the number of ounces by 30.)

1 oz	1/16 lb	30 g
4 oz	¼ lb	120 g
8 oz	½ lb	240 g
12 oz	¾ lb	360 g
16 oz	1 lb	480 g

Useful Equivalents for Cooking/Oven Temperatures

Process	Fahrenheit	Celsius	Gas Mark
Freeze Water	32° F	0° C	
Room Temperature	68° F	20° C	
Boil Water	212° F	100° C	
Bake	325° F	160° C	3
	350° F	180° C	4
	375° F	190° C	5
	400° F	200° C	6
	425° F	220° C	7
	450° F	230° C	8
Broil			Grill

Useful Equivalents for Length

(To convert inches to centimeters, multiply the number of inches by 2.5.)

1 in			2.5 cm	
6 in	½ ft		15 cm	
12 in	1 ft		30 cm	
36 in	3 ft	1 yd	90 cm	
40 in			100 cm	1 m

RECIPE INDEX

A

Alfredo Sauce, 143
Almond Crème, 211
Alysa's Blueberry Pie, 173
Artichoke and Spinach Dip, 229
Avocado Berry Breakfast Boats, 61
Avocado Citrus Parfait, 68
Avocado Lime Sauce, 53

B

Banana Bread, 168
Banana Sushi Rolls, 230
Berries with Hemp Butter, 186
Berry Baskets, 217
Berry Blast-Off, 87
Berry Puree, 182
Blueberry Body & Brain Boost, 92
Breakfast Burrito, Family-Style, 70
Broccoli Pesto Quinoa, 145
Broccoli Poppers, 197
Bugs on a Log, 217

C

Cacao Sauce, 182

Cantaloupe Cups, 74
Cashew Chocolate Sweets, 177
Cheesy Cauliflower, 156
Chia Coconut Fermented Yogurt, 208
Chocolate Chia Pudding, 167
Chocolate Supreme, 84
Cilantro Dressing, 140
Coconut Crème, 67
Coconut Crème Soup, 131
Cookie Bars, 226
Cookies and Tea, 217
Cucumber and Dill Salad, 138
Cucumber Mint, 78

D

Deviled Tomatoes, 153
Dill Pickle Sauerkraut, 210
Doreen's Green Blend, 77
Dylan's Buckwheat Crisps, 187

E

Easy Cookies, 181
Easy Greens, 78
Easy Kale Chips, 198
Easy Wraps, 146
Energy Split-Pea Soup, 127

F

Family 5 Smoothie, 50
Family Flatbread, 117
Fermented-Vegetable Arame Mix, 213
Frozen Fruit Gelato, 221
Fruit and Vegetable Skewers & Snack Shapes, 225
Fruit Salad, 133

G

Gorilla Bowls, 227
Gorilla Greens, 89
Grab-and-Go Breakfast Bars, 60

H

Hummus, 52
Hummus Wraps, 112

L

Laguna Salad, 135
Lentil Soup, 128

M

Mama's Magic Granola, 64–65

Mama's Morning Smoothie, 82
Mango Madness, 86
Mama's Mylk, 244
Mango Vanilla Custard, 194
Marinara Zucchini Sticks, 159
Marvelous Miso Soup, 128
Merry Monkey, 88
Michael's Mushroom Burgers, 104
Mini Apple Cobblers, 178–179
Mint Magic, 94
Miso Soup, 54
Monkey Cereal and Mylk, 71

N

No-Bake Carrot Cake, 166
Nut Butter Bites, 185
Nut-Free Brownies, 174
Nut-Free Trail Mix, 192

O

Orange Sunrise, 91
Orange Turmeric, 77

P

Pink Lemonade, 78
Pumpkin Flax Waffles, 72
Pumpkin Protein Cakes, 109
Pumpkin Seed Bars, 190
Pumpkin Seed Cheese Wraps, 111

Q

Quick Almond Mylk, 88
Quinoa Kidney-Bean Sprouted Veggie Patty, 202–203
Quinoa Protein Pasta, 108

R

Raw Cookie Dough, 170
Raw-Food Candy Boxes, 217
Rawmesan Cheese, 160

S

Savory Tacos, 106–107
Simple Crust, 180
"Smoothie" Bar, The, 220
South of the Border Baked Crisps, Sweet Salsa, and Green Guacamole, 150–151
Sprouted-Buckwheat Snack Mix, 206
Sprouted, Fermented Sesame Mylk, 212
Sprouted-Kamut Bread, 205
Sprouted Lentil Spread, 204
Strawberry Chia Crème, 68
Stuffed Baked Butternut Squash, 155
Stuffed Oranges, 228
Summer Protein Pops, 171
Summer Tacos, 106–107
Sunshine C, 95
Supergreen Goodness, 83
Sweet Cheese, 52
Sweet Ginger Sauce, 142
Sweet Kale Salad, 134
Sweet Pesto, 53
Sweet Pumpkin Butter Spread, 189
Sweet Root-Vegetable Quinoa, 147
Sweet Stuffed Mushrooms, 149
Sweet Tacos, 106–107
Sweet Yams and Rice, 118–119

T

Tahini Cheese Spread, 191
Tahini Sauce, 141
Tangerine Salad, 136
Terrific Tomato, 78
Tomato Basil Bisque, 124
Trail-Mix Cones, 217
Trail Mix Cookies, 193
Tropical Twist, 96
Tuesday Tostadas, 152

V

Vanilla Crunch, 97
Vegetable Minestrone Soup, 130
Veggie Chowder, 126
Veggie Mama Stacks, 115
Veggie Mix, 49
Veggiepalooza, 78
Veggie Tacos with Three Vegetable-Filling Options, 106–107
Veggie-wiches, 114

W

Watermelon Lemonade, 78
Watermelon Pizza Slices, 218
Whipped Avocado in Cucumber Cups, 154

Z

Zoodles of Fun!, 224
Zucchini Noodles, 49
Zucchini Pizza Sticks, 223

Photo of Doreen: Guardian1of7

Photo of Jenny: Fringe Photography

ABOUT THE AUTHORS

Doreen Virtue holds B.A., M.A., and Ph.D. degrees in counseling psychology. A former psychotherapist specializing in eating disorders and addictions, Doreen now gives online workshops on topics related to her books and oracle cards. She's the author of *Assertiveness for Earth Angels, The Miracles of Archangel Michael,* and *Archangel Oracle Cards,* among many other works. She has appeared on *Oprah*, CNN, and *Good Morning America*, and has been featured in newspapers and magazines worldwide. For information on Doreen's work, please visit her at AngelTherapy.com or Facebook .com/DoreenVirtue444. To enroll in Doreen's online video courses, please visit www.Hay HouseU.com and www.EarthAngel.com.

ANGEL THERAPY®

Jenny Ross has been a pioneering spirit of the raw-foods movement since 2000, beginning with her first Los Angeles café. As a chef, she has captivated customers throughout the U.S. with her unique creations. She is the author of four internationally acclaimed wellness titles: *Healing with Raw Foods, Raw Basics, Simple Dehydrated,* and *The Art of Raw Living Foods,* also co-authored with Doreen.

Jenny works with clients of all backgrounds as a holistic nutritionist and health advocate, motivating them toward more vibrant wellness while teaching them about the healing power of living foods. Her award-winning cuisine has drawn a celebrity clientele to her restaurants for over a decade, and her projects have been a positive catalyst for changing many lives in a tangible way. As a wellness expert, she uses her practical knowledge of living raw for over 20 years to create recipes in her restaurants and, more importantly, in her home, as mother to two growing children, Alysa and

Dylan. She currently serves as the director of the International Raw Food Association, connecting raw-foods enthusiasts around the world through raw-foods certification courses, and hosts the Tribestlife YouTube channel *Be Well Kitchen*, offering more easy-to-use recipes and tips on living well in a modern world. Catch Jenny actively teaching classes in the community and online by staying up-to-date at Facebook.com/jennyrosslivingfoods and Instagram.com/jennyrossrawfood.

Website: www.jennyrosslivingfoods.com

♥ ♥ ♥

HAY HOUSE TITLES OF RELATED INTEREST

We hope you enjoyed this Hay House book. If you'd like
to receive our online catalog featuring additional information
on Hay House books and products, or if you'd like to find
out more about the Hay Foundation, please contact:

Hay House, Inc., P.O. Box 5100, Carlsbad, CA 92018-5100
(760) 431-7695 or (800) 654-5126
(760) 431-6948 (fax) or (800) 650-5115 (fax)
www.hayhouse.com® · www.hayfoundation.org

♥

Published and distributed in Australia by: Hay House Australia Pty. Ltd.,
18/36 Ralph St., Alexandria NSW 2015 · *Phone:* 612-9669-4299
Fax: 612-9669-4144 · www.hayhouse.com.au

Published and distributed in the United Kingdom by: Hay House UK, Ltd.,
Astley House, 33 Notting Hill Gate, London W11 3JQ · *Phone:* 44-20-3675-2450
Fax: 44-20-3675-2451 · www.hayhouse.co.uk

Published and distributed in the Republic of South Africa by: Hay House SA (Pty), Ltd.,
P.O. Box 990, Witkoppen 2068 · info@hayhouse.co.za · www.hayhouse.co.za

Published in India by: Hay House Publishers India, Muskaan Complex,
Plot No. 3, B-2, Vasant Kunj, New Delhi 110 070 · *Phone:* 91-11-4176-1620
Fax: 91-11-4176-1630 · www.hayhouse.co.in

Distributed in Canada by: Raincoast Books, 2440 Viking Way,
Richmond, B.C. V6V 1N2 · *Phone:* 1-800-663-5714
Fax: 1-800-565-3770 · www.raincoast.com

♥

Take Your Soul on a Vacation

Visit www.HealYourLife.com® to regroup, recharge, and
reconnect with your own magnificence.
Featuring blogs, mind-body-spirit news, and life-changing
wisdom from Louise Hay and friends.

Visit www.HealYourLife.com today!